Why Did God Let Grandpa Die?

Why Did God Let Grandpa Die?

Phoebe Cranor

DIMENSION BOOKS
BETHANY FELLOWSHIP, INC.
Minneapolis, Minnesota

Why Did God Let Grandpa Die?
by Phoebe Cranor

Library of Congress Catalog Card Number
76-17737

ISBN 0-87123-603-6

Copyright © 1976
Bethany Fellowship, Inc.
All Rights Reserved

Scripture quotations at the end of each chapter are
taken from *The Jerusalem Bible*, copyright © 1966
by Darton, Longman & Todd, Ltd., and Doubleday &
Company, Inc. Used by permission of the publisher.

Published by Bethany Fellowship, Inc.
6820 Auto Club Road,
Minneapolis, Minnesota 55438

Printed in the United States of America

To Susan, Walter, Edith, Alice—
my children

PHOEBE CRANOR is the wife of a cattle rancher. She has nineteen years of experience as a Sunday school teacher. She is a graduate of the Arizona State University and has had stories, poems and articles published through the years.

Preface

I have heard it said, "Teaching teaches the teacher." No truer words were ever spoken, especially when the Teacher of the teacher is the Holy Spirit. This book represents a sequence of my spiritual growing brought to me through my nineteen years of teaching Sunday school and helping rear our own four children. It has been an exciting, frustrating, fast, slow, joyous, painful journey—and I don't think it is over yet. Life gets more exciting and wonderful every minute I live. I hope some of my slowness can be avoided by the parents and teachers who read this book. Perhaps your ears are keener than mine were. Perhaps you are not so stubborn and slow to respond as I was. At any rate, I love the children and am grateful to them for being the vehicle for my own increased awareness of the joy and the power of God's Spirit.

You will notice that different age groups were involved in the following situations. The language for each answer to the children's questions fits the age groups. I didn't try to change that. It seems that children ask certain questions at about the same age; and before that time, they are seldom interested. If your child asks the question, it is very likely that he will be intellectually able to comprehend the answer.

The letter to James (3:1) says, "Only a few of you, my brothers, should be teachers, bearing in mind that those of us who teach can expect a stricter judgement." I am willing to be strictly judged for the sake of my children. However, I know that I have experienced my most tender awareness of the grace of God when I was completely involved in teaching.

Phoebe Cranor

Contents

Chapter 1

Why Did God Let Grandpa Die?

Do I really intend to begin a book for parents and teachers with a chapter on death?

"We must die in order to be born again?"

"We must let go of the old in order for our hands to be free to reach for the new?"

I am beginning with death because that is where my new life began. I had a Sunday school class of kindergartners, as well as four young children of my own. I had thought I was a Christian all my life. In my intellect, I believed. But I belonged to a large group of people who spend hours and dollars not looking at death.

A dead bird would make me glance quickly the other way. I avoided funerals and people whose loved ones had died. I

walled off my own losses quickly and tear-
lessly. And I picked roses just before they
faded in the garden. But once I accidentally
caused the death of a pet cat, and my
tears, endlessly shed, were for all the death
and despair and fear and aloneness that
I would not look at except from around the
corner. I prayed. Haven't we all been
taught to pray? I never looked for the
answers to my prayers, though. That
hadn't been part of my education. "Our
Father who art in heaven. . ." Where's
heaven?

And then one day I came to meet my
Sunday school class of five-year-olds. I
was prepared with lesson plans and art
supplies. I had everything but what I
needed to face a room full of white-faced
children in a trance of stillness and grief.
A young man most of them knew and
loved had been killed in a tragic mishap,
and three of the most sensitive children
had seen it happen.

"God must not have loved him," they
said. "God could have stopped it!" they
cried. "Am I safe?" they whispered. "Was
he bad? Did God punish him? God is
mean. I don't like God." Their anguish expressed every question I had ever pushed
out of my consciousness without an answer.
An hour lay before me to try to help the
children who had been trustingly com-

mitted to my care. Stories and clay and games were useless tools on that day. I prayed what was possibly the first real prayer in my life.

"Oh God, HELP!" Then I sat, my mind blank as two o'clock in the morning, staring into the faces of those beloved, needy, waiting children. And my lips began to move. Words came, bypassing my brain, my own knowledge, my own fear, my limited faith and they reached the children. Like flowers in the rain, they began to brighten. They smiled; they hugged me; they became mischevious. They played and sang and colored. Later, mothers called. "What did you say to them? Tell me, too." Even people I didn't know began calling for help. Pets had died; grandparents were ill; babies had been taken suddenly.

"Oh my God, you care for me. You heard me! I prayed and you answered." What I'd said didn't seem to be coming from me. Yet as I listened to my own voice, my awareness of the love of God was more real than it had ever been before. I had glimpsed into a place of the spirit that I'd only heard of before—and never really believed.

For the Children

There are some things about everybody's houses which are alike. But no two houses are exactly alike. There are some things about all people which are alike. But no two people are exactly alike. They do not look alike and they are not alike inside, either. Let's pretend that your body is your house. It does not look exactly like anyone else's house.

Besides your body, the things that make you be yourself, and not someone else, are the way you think, what makes you laugh, what makes you cry, whom you love, what you like to do, what has happened to you. That is your SELF. This self lives in your house (your body). Billy (or Grandpa, or whoever) lives in his house, too, just as you live in yours. Now let's pretend that one day Billy is happily playing inside his house and a bad storm comes. His house is getting wrecked. Its roof is breaking and its walls are falling down. Billy can't stop his house from being wrecked; but he isn't worried because he has a big, strong, smart daddy who runs in, picks Billy up in his arms, and carries him to a safe place somewhere else. Billy puts his arms tightly around his daddy's neck and you know how safe and happy he feels. He doesn't care where his daddy is taking him. He is just glad to be safe out of the wrecked house.

When someone's house is wrecked so it is no good, God, the Father of us all, takes care of that person. Sometimes we wonder what He did with the person, and sometimes we cry because we're lonely for our loved one who has gone away. But we're never sad or sorry for the friend whom our Father, God, has taken such good care of. We know how much better it is for a person to live where God took him than to have to be sad and uncomfortable in a broken down house.

So when you hear that someone is "dead" and that he is "buried" don't worry. "Dead" means only that his house was no good anymore, and "buried" means that it has been put away in the ground where it will turn into dirt because it isn't any use as a house for anyone's self anymore. The person is safe with his Father God in some other place where he has a better-than-ever dwelling. If the people all around are crying, it is because they know how lonesome they will be to see the person they love. They know that it will be a long time, sometimes, before they wear out their own houses and go to the same place where God has taken Billy.

* * *

If the child who is asking about death does not have a good relationship with his father, it would be wise to change this story

so that whomever he really trusts is substituted for "daddy." If the death was
caused by old age instead of accident, the
story may say that the house had been
used so long that it had become worn out.
Of if the death was caused by illness, it
was a long storm that wrecked the house.
(The child who has lost even an acquaint-
ance from illness will have strange reac-
tions to sickness when it comes to him or
to members of his family for a long time
afterward. He may not express his fears,
but he will need to be reassured often that
people's houses are usually VERY well
built and that his, or his mother's, or whoever, is in very little danger.)

The beloved cat's or dog's house is so
smashed that there is not room for the
self inside to live there. God loves all His
animals too, so we are sure He rescued
the pet. Now we must throw away the
broken house because it is empty and nobody lives there.

Scripture

*Then Peter got out of the boat and started
walking towards Jesus across the water, but as
soon as he felt the force of the wind, he took
fright and began to sink. "Lord! Save me!" he
cried. Jesus put out his hand at once and held
him.* —Matthew 14:29-32

He is God, not of the dead, but of the living.
—Mark 12:27

When this perishable nature has put on imperishability, and when this mortal nature has put on immortality, then the words of scripture will come true: Death is swallowed up in victory. Death, where is your victory? Death, where is your sting?—1 Corinthians 15:54-56

People . . . are in search of their real homeland. They can hardly have meant the country they came from, since they had the opportunity to go back to it; but in fact they were longing for a better homeland. That is why God is not ashamed to be called their God, since he has founded the city for them.—Hebrews 11:14-16

I tell you most solemnly, the hour will come —in fact it is here already—when the dead will hear the voice of the Son of God, and all who hear it will live.—John 5:25

Chapter 2

What Does "Trinity" Mean?

"Father, Son, and Holy Ghost," "filled with the Spirit," "baptism of the Spirit," "speaking in tongues"—these terms all meant the same thing to me. They were abstractions meant for people somehow different from me. I tried to dismiss them. But somewhere, deep inside, there was a longing to know more, to be part of something bigger, if, as I hoped, there really was something.

So one day, I decided (or the Spirit urged me?) to go through my New Testament and mark with an asterisk every mention of the Holy Spirit, by whatever term. Soon my Bible was full of asterisks. "Since I believe in God, since I believe in Jesus Christ," I said to myself, "there must be some explanation for those asterisks."

"There is no explanation," someone told

me. "You just have to accept that part on faith." What part of the knowledge of God does one not accept on faith? Desperately I wanted to believe. "For the promise is to you, and to your children, and to all who are far away..." (Acts 2:39). I was far away.

One day a woman and her children drove into our driveway. I disliked her tremendously, yet I was aware of her desperate need. On impulse I spoke aloud:

"Holy Spirit, if you are real and present today, act through me now." Testing, testing. I knew a moment of guilt at my lack of faith. But what else could I do? I had no button labeled "faith" to push.

True to His nature, the Spirit responded. Bypassing my dislike for the woman, He spoke through me to her needs and she left aglow with joy. For a short moment, I loved her with holy love and was so aware of the Presence that my face felt hot. Sure enough, God's promise was good for me as well as for the early Christians. The power of holiness spread through me with a surge of happiness.

Of course that happiness faded. Of course I forgot to ask and, being a gentleman, the Spirit never forced me. But He did continue to urge me. He did continue to lay situations before me which challenged me to ask Him for His help. And, as often happens in my life, He finally got to me again through children. One Sunday the teacher from the classroom next to me came to my room in tears. The seven-year-olds in her class were in a hot argument with a visiting class about the three persons of the Trinity.

"I can't explain it to them and they are about to fight over it," she wailed. "Help me." She asked me to explain the Trinity to those children. All I knew was that there were dozens of asterisks in my Bible and that I had asked Him twice and had almost forgotten the surge of power and joy of His immediate answer. If ever there was a time to ask for help, I'd come to that time.

"God, help me," I whispered, and then as an afterthought, "give me the power of your Spirit." He did. The presence of the Spirit so filled me that I could almost have touched Him. I sat down on the floor with the two dozen wriggly children and listened to my words tell them what I had never figured out for myself. As usual, when the Spirit spoke through me, the results were entirely satisfying to the children, to the teachers, and apparently to the parents, also, for I was soon asked by several mothers to explain it all to them.

For the Children

Suppose that you had a very busy day.

There were many things to take care of. You wanted to explain to your puppy that you were too busy to play and that you wanted him to help you and that you loved him lots and lots. All your puppy would do was act as if he were afraid of you and feel sad, because he couldn't understand. So you thought about it and decided that if you could make one of your hands into a puppy for a minute, then you could talk in puppy language and explain everything to him and love him too. And at the same time you could go on being yourself and getting your work done.

This is like what God did for people when He sent Jesus. People loved God but there was a lot He wanted to explain to them that they weren't understanding. So He did what we were pretending a minute ago. He made some of himself into a person, a regular man like other men. This wonderful man really could talk to people because He was one of them, but He was God, too, so He knew a lot more about love and teaching and helping people than the rest of us do. Because He was a person, He prayed to God and showed other people how to be what God wanted. But because He was God, too, He was never naughty and mean, and He always loved and understood everyone else. He was himself, like your hand is a separate part of you. Yet He was God, like your hand is still you.

Being a man, though, made Jesus have to do a lot of things that other men do. For example, He had to walk where He wanted to go and could only talk to as many people as could hear His voice at once. There were no microphones or radios, no planes or trains or cars. That made a lot of people not able to see or hear Him. So God had a good plan that took care of all the people who couldn't see Him then, and who wouldn't have been able to see Him since, otherwise. Jesus told the people, "When I have gone back to God, He will send you someone who will give you power from on high. He will send the Holy Spirit." What that meant was that God would send His Spirit to everyone.

His Spirit is just like Jesus except that you can't see Him. He is with everyone at once all over the world just like Jesus was with the people He taught long ago. That is a mystery, which we can't explain. But you know about the Holy Spirit inside yourself just the way you know some other things you can't explain. For example, when you go into the grocery store with your mother, you can be looking at the cereal and she can be buying lettuce on the other side of the store. Yet you know that she is there. You know that she won't leave the store without you. She won't let anyone hurt you, and she probably won't let you do anything naughty while you are there. You are so sure that your mother is there with you that you don't worry about anything—yet you aren't seeing her or hearing her. Or, for another example, suppose you are in bed in your room. Your father or mother or babysitter is in a chair in the living room. You can't see or hear or feel that person. But you are so sure there is a loving person there to take care of you that you go to sleep happy. You know that if you call out, you will be answered and if there is an emergency you are not alone. You know that if you laugh, there is someone to share the joke too, which makes you go to sleep even happier. God's Holy Spirit is ready, also, to help you do hard things or change you if you don't like the way you feel. All you have to do is ask Him. God promised that, and when God promises something, there is no question about His keeping His promise. He always does.

Another interesting thing about the Holy Spirit is that He helps you to realize that Jesus is here, too, and that God loves you. He helps you to know that God and Jesus and the Holy Spirit are very real. They are all here with you just like your mother's head and right hand and left hand are all with you. They are all parts of your mother, yet each one has a separate thing to do and is separate from the others.

It is a very safe and happy life to know that all the parts of God are with you and loving you at once. You can talk to them and they will talk back. Of course, you must learn to listen with your eyes and your ears and your heart. The three persons that God is don't always sound like the voice of your brother or your mother in your ears. Sometimes, if you get to wondering whether or not the Holy Spirit is with you, you can remember a way to check up on Him. Watch for what He is doing. You can't see the wind, but you can tell that the wind is around by what is happening to the trees and the kites, and your cap. You can't see electricity, either, but you know it is there by the fact that when you press the switch, the lights come on. When you ask the Holy Spirit for help, you will get help. That will prove to you that He is there.

Scripture

In the beginning God created the heavens and the earth. Now the earth was a formless void, there was darkness over the deep, and God's spirit hovered over the water.—Genesis 1:1

God said, "Let us make man in our own image . . ."—Genesis 1:26

Here is my servant whom I uphold, my chosen one in whom my soul delights. I have endowed him with my spirit that he may bring true justice to the nations.—Isaiah 42:1

But they rebelled, they grieved his holy spirit.—Isaiah 63:10

. . . but the Advocate, the Holy Spirit, whom the Father will send in my name, will teach you everything and remind you of all I have said to you.—John 14:26

"And now I am sending down to you what the Father has promised. Stay in the city then, until you are clothed with the power from on high."—Luke 24:49

As soon as Jesus was baptised he came up from the water, and suddenly the heavens opened and he saw the Spirit of God descending like a dove and coming down on him. And a voice spoke from heaven, "This is my Son, the Beloved; my favour rests on him."—Matthew 3:16, 17

Chapter 3

How Do We Know
God Hears Us?

I cried out, then, "God is real. He loves
me. He hears me. The Holy Spirit is real
and available to help me. What more can
life offer? It should be bliss and it isn't.
I fail and I'm afraid and I'm moody and
I'm ugly. What is life all about? Nobody
has the answer. Or does Somebody? Perhaps I should ask. And how do I know that
I'm heard and how do I know the answers
to my questions if I am heard? I read the
Bible indifferently and I pray mechani-
cally. And yet I know that God hears. Didn't
He answer my desperate cries and fill me
with His presence before? Of course He
did. I read in the Old Testament about God's
Spirit empowering different people to do
His work. Maybe only when I am actively

engaged in teaching or something similar will He hear my requests."

Lord God, there is nothing so empty as the place you have designed for yourself in our souls. Why does it take some of us so long to realize that you and only you will fit that place? I believed and so I kept on teaching and I kept on calling out to you, "I believe. Help my unbelief." And you kept on answering, waiting until I began to see that all of my life is "your work" if I want it to be, and your work is the filling of my soul with yourself.

And so the other teacher called me and asked me to talk to her third graders about prayer. And again I was asked to go where I wasn't prepared to go. He was one step ahead of me again. I prayed, as before, "Help!" And there I was sitting before a group of children, and I was as engrossed in hearing what I was saying as they were. For outside of my brain, my voice explained what God wanted the children (and me?) to hear about prayer.

For the Children

Do you have a friend that you call on the telephone and talk to? Do you have a friend that you really like so you can say whatever you feel like saying and not worry too much about his or her getting mad? Do you have someone you like enough that sometimes you want to give him or her a present or take him or her on a picnic or to a party? Do you have a friend that you can complain to if you get mad at your mother or your brother, and that you can talk to if you are worried about what someone else is doing? If you have that kind of a friend, you already know a lot about prayer, because God is that kind of a friend, and you can talk to Him in exactly the same way. There is one difference, though. He is always around. The phone never rings and rings without anyone answering it when you want to talk to God, and He is never out playing when you are worried. He is never too busy with His own business to listen, either. God makes a pretty good friend, and because He does, He helps you to be a better friend, too.

God likes for us to see how much He loves us and how much He is doing for us. He wants us to say thank you for what we see. Your other friends like that, too. God likes for us to care for other people. The nice thing about that is that when you tell Him about your worries about someone, and ask Him to, He will get right busy and do something about the problem. Sometimes our other friends don't know how to do anything but feel sorry when someone has trouble. God can *do* things. And when He does, He likes for us to notice and say thank you.

God loves better than anything to do nice things for us. He is just waiting for us to ask Him to come into our lives and start doing things. Sometimes He hears what you want Him to do and knows of something to do that is a lot better than you asked for. If you ever think He hasn't done something that you asked Him to do, look around and see if maybe He has done something a whole lot better than what you asked for. That is often the way He works.

Lots of people talk about praying to God as if they were talking all the time to nobody. The reason they do that is because they have forgotten that when you carry on a conversation with someone, you don't talk all the time. Sometimes you listen to the other person. That is only fair, and if you had a friend you never would let have a word to say, you can be sure you would hear about it from him eventually. He might just stop being friends with you. God will never stop being friends, but He would really like it if you listened to Him once in a while.

How do you hear God? Does His voice come booming out of the sky or the ceiling or something? Well, the interesting thing about the answer to that question is that each person hears God speaking in his own way. A person who is quietly listening will sometimes hear a voice inside his head that tells him that it is God speaking. Another person will just have a feeling inside somewhere that he can't explain. Still another person may read something that just seems to say, "This is a word from God." Even our friends, sometimes, seem to be saying words that came from God through them. We all have to listen and listen to discover how He is going to choose to speak. The good thing is that if we listen carefully, we can always find out.

Some people wonder how to tell if God hears them or not. They are like people who can't hear the dial tone and don't know that the phone is working. Those people won't look for God's answers, and they make it hard for their friends who have talked to God about them. But usually if we watch, we'll see that God does something, eventually, that they can't ignore. We know that He is working. The soft, comfortable way that the pillow feels when we go to bed after talking to God makes us know that He is taking care of things even when we go to sleep and forget about them.

Isn't it something that God takes care of the world and the sky and all the animals and still cares about every person's hurt feelings? Do you ever wonder how He has time for you? If that ever worries you, just remember that if your mother had five children, she would never say, "Oh, I don't care about Billy. I have four other children.

I don't need him." Somehow, you know that if Billy were floating down the river, his mother would run and pull him out—even if she did have four other children. Well, suppose she had six children, or seven, or ten, or even twelve. She would still love Billy as much as ever. God has more children than that, of course, but He still loves every single one just as much as the others. And nobody who loves you will do things to hurt you or not care what happens to you.

Scripture

Call to me and I will answer you; I will tell you great mysteries of which you know nothing. —Jeremiah 33:3

If you ask for anything in my name, I will do it.—John 14:14

Be happy at all times; pray constantly; and for all things give thanks to God, because this is what God expects you to do in Christ Jesus. —1 Thessalonians 5:17

Chapter 4

Why Did Jesus Have to Die?

"Why did Jesus have to die? He could have saved himself. God could have saved Him. God was mean to let Him die." Children of all ages have thought they couldn't believe in a God who would let His own Son die. And who was I to try to explain to the children about the sacrificial death of our Lord on the cross? But talking to God in the way I had heard Him telling me through my ministry to the children was making me aware that there is more to belief than intellectual ideas.

The Holy Spirit was doing for me what I had done many times to make friends with a stranger. He was helping me with the dishwashing and other tasks of daily living so that I could get acquainted with Him as a person. At first I self-consciously asked Him for His help. At first I tested His presence and thanked Him uncomfortably, as we do newly discovered friends. But He knew what He was doing. He kept leading and guiding and giving me the right books to read, so that I began to feel that He was more and more a part of my life. I felt His presence at my side more and more often and with less and less self-consciousness on my part. I treasured moments of the beautiful awareness of holiness and used those moments to bolster my own need to be self-sufficient. I could teach, couldn't I? God often spoke to me through my teaching. I took His presence during the moments of teaching as my sign that I was using my gifts and doing what He wanted me to do. And I am sure that I was. But it was a long time after He gave me my first hint of the magnificence of His presence before I dared to look at the gift of His sacrifice full in the face.

One day a group of fifth graders were hot in an argument about the sacrificial death of Jesus. Their teacher asked me for help. I didn't understand with my brain, but how my heart longed to know.

"Dear Lord, answer these children's questions through me again," I cried, never realizing that He was answering the ultimate question of my own life when He spoke through me to the children.

For the Children

A long time ago God told the people that He knew they had a hard time being good. He told them that He realized that they might not always want to be bad but that they sometimes couldn't seem to help it. You know that yourself. Sometimes you just feel so ugly that you do bad things even when you wish you wouldn't. If we keep on being bad and being bad when we really don't want to again and again, after awhile it almost makes us sick, we feel so sad. It's like badness gets piled up higher and higher in our insides until we just nearly burst. God knew that about His people. So He gave those long-ago people something they could do about it. He told them that, since our blood is the most important thing inside us, He'd let blood be a sign to them that He had heard them saying they were sorry for their badness. Only instead of their own blood, He'd let them use the blood of animals. That sounds pretty awful to us, but He did it for a sign to the people that they could see and understand.

God told the people that just any animal's blood wouldn't do. The animal had to be a certain kind, as well as perfect: the very best one that a person had. It had to be, in fact, an animal that the person might want most of all to keep. People were poor enough, mostly, that it was hard to give away the best animal. But it had to be something special given to God in order to be a real reminder to the person that God had forgiven them of all their badness. It took a lot of animals, because people had to keep doing it every time they were bad. That way of remembering God's forgiveness lasted for a long, long time.

All during this long, long time, God kept telling His people that He was going to give them another way to remember that they were forgiven. In fact, He was going to give them another way to be forgiven—a new way not using animals at all. (We call it "prophecy" when we talk about those hints of something new that was coming.) And after a while, sure enough, the new way came into the world. That new way was Jesus. He started out as a baby, as you know, and He grew and grew. Jesus was a person, like we are, but He was also God. We talked in another class about how your hand is a part of you, and it isn't all of you, and it is separate from you—all at once. Remember that Jesus was God and a person at the same time, just as your hand is a hand and not something else, and still it is part of you. So when He grew up He was still God and was perfect, but He was still a man telling people a lot of things about God. He said to the people that if they would believe that He was really God, they would see by the way He acted what God is like. He was so loving and kind and knew so many wonderful things that the people who knew Him loved Him with all their hearts. They had a whole new idea of how good and loving God is from being around Jesus.

The people who were around Jesus and loving Him didn't know it, but He was getting ready to show them the new way of being forgiven. A lot of the men who were important in the church were afraid of Jesus. They thought too many people were following Him and that He was going to become a king and make a lot of trouble for them. The people were living in a land that already had a leader that was like a king. The leader wouldn't have liked for a little bunch of people to start following someone else and calling him their king. So the men in the church decided it would be a good idea to get rid of Jesus. They decided to kill Him. What Jesus did, you see, was to use His own blood instead of animal blood to pay for all the bad things people had always done and were still doing—and also were surely going to do in the future—to sort of stand in for all the badness, and pay everyone's fines, and remind everyone that God had forgiven them forever. As a lawyer friend once said, "Jesus told the judge that even if the man on trial was guilty and should be hung for his crime, Jesus would be hung instead so the man could go free." He said that to every person in the world about everything bad he had ever done. And He said it to all the people since then, because God loves everyone all the time.

Sure enough, you know, Jesus was killed. In fact, He had the very worst, most hurting kind of death people could think of to give Him. It was a terrible time for all the people who loved Him. He had died and they thought that He was gone forever. (But God had other ideas.) To be hanging naked on a cross where He had been put with big nails was the worst thing that could be done to Jesus. And even worse was the fact that a lot of the people who loved Him for a little while forgot about it and laughed at Him hanging there in front of them in the sun. God let this happen to Jesus, who was, you know, like your hand is to you—a part of God himself—because He knew that Jesus wasn't going to have to stay dead. He knew that He would rise from being dead and be alive again. This was a miracle which God gave us to show that He is greater than the very worst badness that men can think of. He told us, when He made Jesus not dead after He had been dead, that even being dead doesn't separate us from God. It also showed the people that no matter how bad they had been, if they were sorry and asked God to, He would remember Jesus' blood and take away the badness without any more blood, ever. Jesus took all the bad with Him when He died, and when He came back to life, the badness wasn't with Him.

Now, Jesus' doing that didn't make us so we'll never be bad again. And it didn't make us free to be bad every time we want to, either. If someone showed you that good is a lot bigger and better than bad, you would hardly choose bad. Who wants to be on the losing side? But when people believe in Jesus and love Him, they know that when they make a mistake and do something bad, He has already showed them that God will forgive them. Not only that, when we tell God that we are sorry we have been bad, He doesn't just forgive the badness. He also takes it and makes something good out of it. That is really exciting. Nobody can feel all full of badness and be unhappy when he knows that God is making it into good. We never need to forget that Jesus used His blood to show us that goodness is *always* bigger than badness, forever and forever. Nobody can really understand how very much God loves us until he starts being a friend of Jesus and sees for himself what God is like.

Scripture

*And yet ours were the sufferings he bore, ours the sorrows he carried. But we, we thought of him as someone punished, struck by God, and brought low. Yet he was pierced through for our faults, crushed for our sins. On him lies a punishment that brings us peace, and through his wounds we are healed. We had all gone astray like sheep, each taking his own ways, and Yahweh burdened him with the sins of all of us. Harshly dealt with, he bore it humbly, he never opened his mouth, like a lamb that is led to the slaughterhouse, like a sheep that is dumb before its shearers, never opening its mouth. By force and by law he was taken; would anyone plead his cause? Yes, he was torn away from the land of the living; for our faults struck down in death. They gave him a grave with the wicked, a tomb with the rich, though he had done no wrong and there had been no perjury in his mouth. Yahweh has been pleased to crush him with suffering. If he offers his life in atonement, he shall see his heirs, he shall have a long life and through him what Yahweh wished will be done. His soul's anguish over he shall see the light and be content. By his sufferings shall my servant justify many, taking their faults on himself.—*Isaiah 53:4-12

*Was it not ordained that the Christ should suffer and so enter into his glory?—*Luke 24:26

*The Father loves me, because I lay down my life in order to take it up again. No one takes it from me; I lay it down of my own free will. . . . —*John 10:17-18

We must realise that our former selves have been crucified with him to destroy this sinful body and to free us from the slavery of sin. . . . But we believe that having died with Christ we shall return to life with him.—Romans 6:6-9

A man can have no greater love than to lay down his life for his friends.—John 15:12

Chapter 5

What Is Communion For?

The clink of little glasses in the hall outside the Primary Room caught the children's attention. We took a trip out to watch the ladies pour the wine into tiny glasses and pile the little squares of bread onto silver plates. It looked like fun and magic and a party.

"Can we have some, too?" the children begged. "What is it for?"

What is it for? Did I know? In a moment of awful self-awareness, I realized that I had "taken communion" for a lifetime without really knowing what it was all about. And if I could go for a lifetime without knowing what it was about, how could these primary children ever know? Their eager faces turned toward me. "Become as little children," I thought. Why shouldn't we learn together what communion means? Why shouldn't I ask the One who had unfailingly led my voice before to lead me again? We went inside the room.

On the floor with the children I realized that we all have the puzzle of magic. "Jesus was magic," a hundred children had said to me. "Jesus did tricks." Yes, Jesus is magic. He is magic if one defines "magic" as being in the heart of Things Eternal and being moved by the power of that same Eternal. But Jesus is not magic if magic becomes using and manipulating and tricking. Children have a natural loathing of being tricked. They quickly sense the difference between manipulative trickery and the magic of the Eternal and ever-present fairyland which they love. All good witches can create, but bad witches can only destroy. I believe that many children are turned away from the real and loving Father God because their elders fail to do away with the "Jesus can do tricks" fallacy when it first arises in some poorly presented story of His life and teachings.

And so I asked for the magic of God's love and the truth of His revelation and the words to tell about Eucharest without knowing that I was at last asking what the Holy Spirit had been waiting for me to ask: for Him to leave off working *beside* me and begin working *in* me.

For the Children

People in churches all over the world do something that we call Eucharest or Communion. They have little glasses of either juice or wine and little pieces of bread or cracker to eat together in the church. The minister or priest prays about it and all the people eat and drink. Let's see what the bread and wine are for.

Blood is very important in the body of any animal or person. It is so important that long, long ago God told His people that when they had been bad, they must pour out some blood to show that they were sorry. He didn't make them use their own blood, though. He had them use the blood from a perfect animal, one that they would like best of all to keep. It was as if you put your badness on the perfect animal and gave the animal to God by killing it. The blood of the animal washed away your badness and reminded you that God had forgiven you. Later, Jesus took the place of all the animals and used His own blood to say "I'm sorry" in place of all the people who did bad things. He had to die to do it, and it was a big gift to give all of His blood that way. It was as if all the people were saying "I'm sorry" at once. When people say that "Jesus died for our sins," it means that when He died in that terrible way on the cross, all our badness and things we're sorry for died with Him. It's like all of the people, including you and me, tying all of our bad actions and feelings up in a big bundle and giving it to Him so He could take it with Him when He died. Then when He rose up and was alive again, He left our badness behind. We can do bad things again, of course, but if we love Jesus, we know He will say to us, "You aren't bad. You just did a bad thing. I know you are sorry, so don't cry. I have thrown your badness away and God has forgiven it."

Jesus lived and died and came to life again a long time ago. But once He came to life, He stayed alive. The Bible says He went to be with God as if you moved your hand from under the table and put it behind your head. But he left us the Holy Spirit, which is like God's other hand, to look after us and be with us all the time.

Now the idea of eating and drinking is this: when we eat and drink, we open our mouths and take something inside of us. We know that a cookie sitting on the table won't get us over being hungry unless we open our mouths and bite into it and swallow it. We know that the power of God which Jesus showed us while He was here, and which the Holy Spirit shows us whenever we ask Him to, is here with us. But we need to do something to get that inside of us. The power of Jesus using His blood to say "I'm sorry" for our badness isn't in the little glass of juice or wine. The power comes when we use the wine to say to God, "See, I'm ready to open up and take something inside of me." And what is that something? It is that you know God has forgiven you and loves you and wants you to love Him. The little bread or cracker pieces that we eat are saying to God, "See, I want the power and love of Jesus and the Holy Spirit to be inside of me from now on." When the priest says, "The body and blood of our Lord and Savior, Jesus Christ" as he hands you the bread and the wine, he means that as soon as you open your mouth and take those things in and swallow them, you are going to have God's forgiveness and power and Jesus' love inside you. People like to do that over and over again because they don't ever want to forget how great it is to never be lonesome for God because His Spirit is inside them.

There is one more thing about Communion. People like to eat together. They like to talk and laugh together. Notice how we always have food at a party? So when we open up to God by eating bread and drinking wine, we like to do it together. We talk about Jesus and tell both what He does for us and what we can do for Him. And He brings a present to the party, too, for everyone. What present? God's power and love and happiness inside of us. Isn't that a big present? Part of Communion, just like part of any other party, is saying thank you for the present. And the bigger the present, the bigger the thank you needs to be.

Scripture

And as they were eating he took some bread, and when he had said the blessing he broke it and gave it to them. "Take it," he said, "this is my body." Then he took a cup, and when he had returned thanks he gave it to them, and all drank from it, and he said to them, "This is my blood, the blood of the covenant, which is to be poured out for many."—Mark 14:22-25

The blessing-cup that we bless is a communion with the blood of Christ, and the bread that we break is a communion with the body of Christ.—1 Corinthians 10:16

Chapter 6

Why Does God Allow Suffering?

Maybe the last great hurdle we have to leap in the journey through to faith is the hurdle of pain and suffering. Nobody, old or young, can truly believe until his heart has opened enough to let in the suffering of the world. Nobody who is truly yearning after God can say His will is for us to suffer. It wasn't until I saw that God's love was a circle larger than the suffering, and surrounding it, that I could begin to know the meaning of love. I put up a barrier to the entrance of the Holy Spirit into my inner self until this problem was solved. God commanded us to praise Him no matter what happened. "Praise Him for ugliness?" I said. "Praise Him for suffering and death, for the pain of the innocent?" I said. "I won't." But one morning I realized that that command was God's gift. It was our tool for rising above the suffering that errant humanity had caused for the innocent and the guilty alike. It was a tool for seeing the goodness and love and mercy of God in spite of suffering...or because of it. It was the only way to participate in the love of God. Praising Him for His very presence was the key that opened the door to my last reserve and allowed me to let God inside. The Holy Spirit *with* me is a sometime experience but the Holy Spirit *in* me is forever.

But this hadn't happened yet when I was forced to tell my children why one of them had to be sick or hurt or why there were children in India who "looked awful" because they were dying of hunger. The barrier was still there, and I had no idea how to leap over it.

"Dear Lord, you've been helping me with this teaching for a long time. This is the first time I've ever dared let them ask me the ultimate question. If I let them ask me today, will you provide the answer? It isn't dying that I'm faced with, God. It's the whole problem of evil and meaninglessness and the ultimate nothingness that is worse than death. Help me again, I pray." And He did. The answer to this question was the key to the final "letting go" that He was waiting to give me—waiting for nearly fifty years.

For the Children

Some people get mad at God because He lets other people and animals get hurt and die. You know how you feel sometimes when something bad happens to your friend and it just wasn't fair at all. You say, "If God loved that person, He'd never let bad things happen to him." And you feel so mad at God you'd like to spit in His face. God understands how you feel. Nearly everyone feels that way sometimes. Lots of things don't seem fair. God knows that. He is sorry right along with you when something makes you sad. Then why doesn't He stop all that bad stuff that is happening?

If you wanted to do something and someone stopped you, you wouldn't like it. Supposing you decided to learn to ride a two-wheeler bike but your mother told you you couldn't do it because you'd fall and hurt yourself. That would really make you mad. You would like it a lot better if she let you ride, even though you fell off a lot of times and had blood and bruises all over. You would also like it if your mother put a band-aid on the sore spots and praised you for learning to ride. You could thank her for the bike and be glad you were getting to be a good rider and that your mother was your good friend who loved you and helped you and maybe eventually went bike riding with you somewhere on a picnic.

God is like that, too. He could make us into puppets on a string and never let us do anything but what He wanted us to. But He knows that we will be happier if we have a chance to choose what we do. He knows that some of us will make very bad choices and hurt ourselves and other people, and that sometimes those other people will not have done a thing to deserve it— like if you hit your little brother while you were learning to ride your bike. Or maybe you ran right over your puppy's tail and broke it off so he would never have a tail again. Even though those bad things happened, you would still be glad that you had a chance to learn to ride a bike. God loves us very much and He would like for us all to choose the very best things that there are for ourselves. In fact, He wants most of all for us to *choose* to ask Him what we should do and then do it. But He made a rule that He was going to let each one of us decide, and He won't break that rule. He won't break it for the boy learning to ride a bike and He won't break it if a man decides to shoot someone or something else mean that causes a lot of trouble. God is really fair when He gives us free choice.

Besides giving us a choice, though, He has given us something else. He has told us that when we make a bad choice and mess things up, we can come and ask Him

to help us and He will. If we make such
a mess that we can't get out of it, He will
still love us and forgive us and get us out
of the mess. He will even help the people
we have hurt. However, He likes for us to
ask Him. He gave us free choice, and He
will wait for us to ask Him to be rescued
when we need to be.

Now you are maybe wondering about
things like hurricanes and earthquakes,
which nobody chose to have and nobody
understands. That question is harder. But
a man named Paul, who listened to God
very carefully, heard Him say that everything in the world gets sort of messed up
by so many people choosing to do the wrong
things and hurting each other and the
world. The whole world is, along with God
himself, waiting for everyone to choose to
love God and ask Him for help. In the mean-
time, He still helps and loves us all. If we
ask Him to, He makes the bad things that
happen, even a hurricane, turn out to be
good things. He's like Mother when you are
learning to ride a bike. She will give you
such a special loving when you fall and
hurt yourself that you think it was almost
worth getting hurt to have her show you
so much love. And of course, when you feel
loved, then you try harder to love other
people and to choose right instead of wrong
things. God said that someday everyone

would love Him and choose good. We don't see that happening yet, but each one of us can help it happen by asking God to tell us what He'd like for us to do.

Scripture

We know that we belong to God, but the whole world lies in the power of the Evil One. —1 John 5:19

From the beginning till now the entire creation, as we know, has been groaning in one great act of giving birth. . . .—Romans 8:22

We know that by turning everything to their good, God co-operates with all those who love him. . . .—Romans 8:28

For I am certain of this: neither death nor life, no angel, no prince, nothing that exists, nothing still to come, not any power, or height or depth, nor any created thing, can ever come between us and the love of God made visible in Christ Jesus our Lord.—Romans 8:38-39

Chapter 7

Why Do We Have the Bible?

The third graders next door were having a real argument about the Bible. Parroting their parents' ideas and prejudices, they were in the same state of heat-without-light that grown people often find themselves. My kindergartners and their helper were deep in a construction project, so I went over to assist.

"Father, help me," I prayed. "Help me to be alive to what you would have these children hear as a pattern for their future."

In the instant before I opened the door, my own life flashed before me. My own feelings about God's Holy Word ran a quick panorama, and I gasped at the realization of the changes the Holy Spirit had produced in my understanding of it. And I saw that we can find in the Bible whatever we look for. The historian can find history and he can, with practiced eye, ignore the Person who is responsible for the history. The scientist can find the rudiments of science as we know it; the physician can find the rules of health. The writer can find plots and the seeker of excitement can find thrills. The seer can find signs, and even the doubter can find the blood and pain that he wants to see to feed his doubting. There is whatever we look for, but there is always more. There is always the love which is, as in all of life, an invisible force with visible results.

The Book in my hand seemed alive with the love which is God's revelation of himself.

"My Book is a letter," the Spirit seemed to be saying to me, "a letter with your name on every page."

For the Children

Before we talk about the Bible, let's pretend something. Let's pretend that you have gotten a letter from your friend, Billy. Billy writes: "I have a new pony. My daddy gave him to me for my birthday. He gave me a new red saddle and bridle and he built a shed for the pony. He put in a 100-pound sack of grain for him, too. The first time I tried to ride, the saddle was not tight enough. I fell off and hurt my arm. My daddy put a bandage on my arm and then he fixed the saddle. He helped me get on and I rode all morning. I am happy."

Now if you are Billy's friend, you will surely be glad to hear all those good things about the new pony. You will be interested that Billy fell off and glad that his daddy was there to fix his arm and to tighten the saddle. But let's pretend again. Let's pretend that another friend of yours and his family are thinking about moving to live next door to Billy's family. The father comes to you and says, "Tell me about Billy's daddy. We are going to be neighbors and I want to know what kind of man he is." You might go get your letter from Billy to show the man. Now let's see what we can figure out from Billy's letter about what kind of a daddy he has.

First, he is a very loving daddy to give Billy a gift like a pony. We can see that he is a thoughtful daddy who knows that a boy needs a saddle and a bridle and a shed and a bag of grain as well as just the pony. We can see that he cares about the future and knows that the pony will need a lot of grain to eat. We might guess that he is pretty rich, since ponies, sheds, grain, and saddles cost lots of money.

Another thing we might notice is that Billy's daddy can build, since Billy said he built a shed. And he can fix things, since Billy mentioned that he knew how to tighten the saddle and to bandage his arm. We might also notice that he stayed around to make sure Billy was going to ride all right, so he was a daddy who cared. He must have been very interested in all the things that happened to his son, since he spent all that time with Billy.

See how much we found out about Billy's father just from reading a letter from Billy about what had happened to him? That is the way it is with the Bible. Sometimes you wonder if God wrote the Bible or not. Well, He didn't write the Bible with a big pen that came down from a cloud in the sky. But in a way He wrote it by letting the facts that He wanted us to know come out in what people wrote. And just as it was with Billy's letter, the important things about Billy's father were all in the letter when we looked.

Now some people think of the Bible as mostly a book of rules. Let's pretend again. What are some of the good rules we could make from Billy's letter? Rule No. 1 might be "Ponies need food." Rule No. 2: "Ponies need sheds." Rule No. 3 might be "Saddles should be fastened carefully before riding ponies." We could also say, "Hurts should be bandaged." These are good rules. But when Billy wrote to you and told you about his pony, he wasn't writing you a rule book. He was just telling you what had happened

to him. Still, those good ideas are all there
if you want to look for them. The Bible
is like that, too. We can find all sorts of
good rules to live by if we read carefully.
But the Bible isn't just a rule book. Just
like Billy's letter, it tells us about other
people and ourselves (because we can
imagine so well what Billy felt like when
he got the pony and when he fell and when
his daddy helped him and when he finally
did ride). And it tells us things about God
just the way Billy's letter told us about his
daddy. It tells us lots of good rules and
ideas about the best way to live, too.

The next question most people ask is
why the Bible is the size it is. God never
stops doing things for people and lots has
happened since it was written. That is a
good question. To answer it, let's take another look at Billy's letter. There are a lot
of things happening to Billy that he didn't
tell us in his letter. We might like to know
them, too. What is his teacher's name?
How big is his bedroom? What kind of
weather is there where he lives? What
color is his bicycle? But Billy wrote in his
letter what he wanted to tell us. Wishing
he had told us more doesn't do us much
good because the letter is as long as he
wanted to make. it. That is the way the
Bible is, too. As we said before, God didn't
take a big pencil and send it down out of

the clouds to write the Bible. But He was responsible for it, just the same, by making the people who wrote it want to write what was important. Whatever is necessary for us to know is in the Bible somewhere and we can find it if we look. The more carefully we study it the more of what we need to know we will find in it. It is just like Billy's letter was. If we look carefully at what he said and think about everything that we can figure out from what is there, we have a lot of information.

Now there might be one more hard question. Lots of grown-ups are interested in what they call "prophecy" and that sounds a bit scary. And some people are afraid, too, although they don't need to be at all. Prophecy is a sort of seeing what is happening or is going to happen from the signs. There is a prophecy in our letter from Billy. Can you guess what it is? Well, I'll tell you. Billy's father bought a 100-pound sack of grain for the pony. If you have ever fed a pony, you know that he eats mostly grass and you only give him a little bucketful of grain a day. A 100-pound sack is a lot of grain. The pony will not finish it off for days and days. What is the prophecy? It is that Billy's daddy intends to keep the pony for quite a long time. Now we might wonder if that means that we will sell the pony when the grain is gone. But there is another prophecy in the letter, too. Daddy built a shed for the pony. Sheds last a long, long time—much longer than a sack of grain. If he were planning to sell the pony in a month, say, it doesn't seem logical for Billy's daddy to go to the trouble of building a solid long-lasting shed, does it? There are several books in the Bible, and especially the last one, Revelation, that tell us a lot about the signs of what God is going to do. Some people spend their time trying to figure out exactly what is going to happen and when. That is all right if they don't worry about it. It would be too bad if Billy got so worried about how long his daddy was going to keep the pony that he forgot how nice it was to have it or what a good daddy he had who gave it to him in the first place.

We love to read the Bible for lots of reasons. The best reason, though, is to find out how well He loves us and how happy it can make us to know the best, richest, kindest Daddy that Billy and you and I have: God.

Scripture

All scripture is inspired by God and can profitably be used for teaching, for refuting error, for guiding people's lives, and teaching them to be holy. This is how the man who is dedicated to God becomes fully equipped and *ready for any good work.—*2 Timothy 3:16-17

*You are new born, and, like babies, you should be hungry for nothing but milk—the spiritual honesty which will help you to grow up to salvation—now that you have tasted the goodness of the Lord.—*1 Peter 2:2-3

. . . he who rejects me and refuses my words has his judge already: the word itself that I have spoken will be his judge on the last day. —John 12:48

Chapter 8

What Is a Love Blanket?

"A little child shall lead them."

One year there were eighteen boys and three girls in my kindergarten class. We were short of space and short of materials. One of the girls had a severe hearing loss and one of the boys had a destructive emotional problem. If I hadn't realized the power and presence of the Holy Spirit, that class would have finished my Sunday school teaching abruptly. Instead, it became the vehicle for some of my own best growing experiences.

So often I forget the ever-present resource of asking for help. Pride, I guess, gets in the way. "I can handle it," I say to myself. But I can't. On my own, I am less capable than I used to be—or I am more aware of the potential in each situation. In any case, the Sunday that we discovered the "love blanket," the Holy Spirit was speaking and His voice sounded surprisingly like Jennifer's. Our emotionally disturbed boy had lunged at another child with a pair of open scissors, and I had scooped him up just the second before the scissors made contact. I was holding him close, singing to him, and the other children were standing, waiting for the next activity.

"Sit down," I said, suddenly. "Let's ask Jesus what we can do for Bob." We sat quietly for a minute before Jennifer spoke. Holding out her hands in a mother's gesture of comfort, she said, "Let's wrap him in a love blanket." It was as if at that moment a real blanket came down over us. The children snuggled together, smiling. Even the active poking-each-other subsided. Twenty wriggly five-year-olds sat in silence looking at each other with awe on their faces.

"Thank you, Jesus," I said and we began to talk the love blanket. It has become a very real part of my life, and I believe is forever present in the lives of those children. The "ok child" of Thomas Harris responds to the love blanket instinctively, the "not-ok child" reaches for it, and the "nurturing parent" holds it out. Thank you, Jesus.

For the Children

Do you know what is all around us

right now—both inside the house and outside? It is air, isn't it? But we can't see it. We can't touch it, either. God's love is all around us, too, like the air. We can't see it or touch it. We know it is there because He told us that in the Bible. But sometimes we forget about love and act as if it weren't there at all. When things are wrong and we are unhappy or sick, and when other people are grumpy and unpleasant, we forget that love is everywhere. That is the time we are glad that we know about the love blanket.

Let's imagine that there is a blanket in the room here with us. Think of the most furry, soft, warm blanket you have ever seen and the prettiest color you know. Pretend it is wrapped around you and you can feel it with your arms and legs and against your face. Pretend you pull it close and it even smells nice. Rub it with your nose and curl your toes in it. Doesn't it make you feel good? Now pretend that you have just come in from the snow and are all cold and tired. Wrap up in the blanket and feel how good and warm you are. This is God's love blanket. It is what the Holy Spirit gives us to let us feel love. Whenever you especially need to feel love like you feel someone touching you, there is the love blanket to pull around yourself.

Of course, there are lots of times when

everyone needs to have that feeling of love. Imagine how it is when you have an earache. A warm, soft blanket pulled against your ear makes it better. Or imagine being very sad and lonely. When you pull that warm blanket around you and cry against it, you are suddenly all well and happy again. Or when someone has scolded you, you can get your blanket and wrap in it, and all at once you are sorry you were bad and it is all over and well again, so you are loving and happy. The Holy Spirit gave you that blanket to help you when you have any kind of trouble.

There is something else that the blanket is good for, too. Sometimes it isn't you who is having trouble. A while ago, one of our boys was feeling unhappy. He felt all alone and he wanted to hurt someone. And maybe he didn't know about the love blanket. That was the time for someone else to come running and wrap it around him. It is a very loving thing to wrap someone up with a warm, soft, safe, happy blanket. It takes a lot of the hurt away, no matter what hurts.

Suppose, though, that someone has hurt you and made you mad. And maybe you don't want him to feel good and loved. Maybe you'd rather he felt bad for a while to serve him right. Everyone feels like that sometimes. God knows that. He knows how mad we can get and how we'd really like to hurt someone back when he has hurt us first. So He lets the Holy Spirit start quietly whispering to us. He whispers love thoughts that somehow remind us of the love blanket even if we don't want to think about it. And pretty soon, even if we didn't mean to feel like it, we find ourselves going after the love blanket to wrap someone up in. That's fun. It is always fun to surprise another person. If you were really mad a minute ago and then you got over it and came with a blanket of love, that is a real surprise. That makes the person you were mad at so surprised that before long you both laugh because you can't help it. Love blankets are full of laughing. They are full of surprises. Your love blanket never gets dirty or messed up or wrinkled. It is never folded away on a shelf where you can't reach it. Yours is right with you wherever you are so you can reach out and get it whenever you need it. Put out your hand right now and let's pull all the love blankets in this room close around everyone. Isn't that a good feeling?

Scripture

Hatred provokes disputes, love covers over all offenses.—Proverbs 10:12

I give you a new commandment: love one another; just as I have loved you, you also must love one another.—John 13:34

May the Lord be generous in increasing your love and make you love one another and the whole human race as much as we love you. —1 Thessalonians 3:12

No one has ever seen God; but as long as we love one another God will live in us and his love will be complete in us. —1 John 4:12

Chapter 9

What Is Sin?

"You're sinning. You lied!"

"I'm not sinning. What is sinning?"

Fifth graders have a very much black-and-white outlook toward life. The young-sters were heatedly discussing all the things I had wondered about sin: where did it come from and what is it and how do we know we are involved? They were hot and frustrated, their parents' defenses all hang-ing out in their arguments.

Some of the more sophisticated mem-bers of our society may feel, honestly, that the concept of sin is outdated. However, their children have some sort of instinctive intuition that it is there. They are so near, I guess, to the source of all life that the basic facts of their existence are present inside them—and not so far from the sur-face as the same facts in their parents' lives. Tales of witches and black magic have a ring of truth in them for our children, and therein rests their ever-present danger. Truly I had a good opportunity here to give my friends, the fifth graders, some of the tools with which to battle the evil of the world.

But in our Community Church there are so many philosophies represented that if I approached the problem logically I would be sure to offend someone. "Father, help me, please."

There is no doubt about it, "help" is my favorite prayer. When I am totally at a loss about anything, I find that God answers my prayer of simply "help!" the most quickly. And I find, too, that I feel a peace and security about my answers when I haven't known at all what I should say.

So I shut my eyes, so to speak, and jumped into a discussion of sin.

For the Children

A long, long time ago, before this world was even made, God gave all the angels a chance to choose whether or not to love Him. Some of the angels decided not to, so they turned away from God and started doing what they wanted to apart from God. You have all heard the story about Adam and Eve in the Garden of Eden. Remember that the trouble all started when the snake told Eve to do something God had told her He didn't want her to do. The problem was not what Eve did as much as that she was doing what she wanted to do instead of what God wanted her to do.

To see how this works out, let's pretend that you are quite small and you have gone to the grocery store with your mother. She has told you to stay right beside her. She has given you a sucker to eat and a little book to look at so you will be happy. But you decide you want to see what you can find in the aisle she has just passed. So you take a few steps into it away from your mother. You haven't really done anything wrong at all. All you have done is gone away from her. But as soon as you are away from your mother, you see a toy on the shelf, so you go on up and look at it. Your mother is probably watching you and knows what you are doing, but you have almost forgotten about her while you are so busy.

In a little while, you see something else and you wander farther and farther until pretty soon you feel as if you aren't in the store with your mother at all, but are there all alone. And after a long, long while, you might get to feeling that you didn't even have a mother at all. That would be pretty scarey, and about then you would probably start to cry and someone would help you to find your mother again and get back to her where you belonged.

This picture of you in the grocery store is a pretty good picture of what sin is. It is deciding to go off on your own away from God. After you go away from Him you start doing things you shouldn't do and getting farther and farther from caring what He thinks. But the things you are doing aren't making you get far from God. Getting far from God is what makes you feel as if you can do whatever you want to.

Remember we started out talking about the angels? Maybe you are right now wondering what angels have to do with the little boy in the grocery store. This is the answer. Lucifer was God's best angel to start with. His name means "Son of Light." So when he decided to stop loving God and started doing things for himself alone and loving himself instead of God, he couldn't stay in heaven anymore. Some of the other angels decided to be like him and they couldn't stay in heaven any more either. When God made this earth, Lucifer and his followers came here to live. This is the story . in the Bible that explains why we are bad when we wish we weren't and why we are often unhappy and miserable. Lucifer became what we call "Satan" or the "Devil" or just "evil," and all those other fallen angels became his little helpers. Some people say that Satan isn't real—that he and his little helpers are all just made up. Satan likes for them to think that because then he can go around getting people to do bad things and they won't know what is happening. When Adam and Eve listened to the snake, they were really listening to the devil. And lots of times when we sin, we are listening to him, too. Sometimes we don't even realize what we are doing—and he likes that.

There is another important thing to know about sin. It is that Jesus is bigger than the devil and all the bad ideas he can put into our heads. Jesus beat the devil when He let himself be killed on the cross and then came back to life again. He showed the devil that there was nothing in the world or in heaven either that would win in any argument with Jesus. So sin—every kind of badness that comes from forgetting God—is smaller than Jesus. When any kind of bad thoughts or feelings come into us, all we have to do is just say, "Jesus, help me," and the devil has to leave. He likes to bother us and try to make us sin, but he can't live where Jesus is or stand hearing the name of Jesus, even.

You may be wondering something that most people wonder at one time or another. That is why the mother in the grocery store didn't just hold on tightly to that little boy and not let him go and do what he wanted to. Think how you felt when you were smaller and your mother did hold tightly to you and not let you go somewhere or do something. You didn't like it a bit. You felt angry at her and maybe even kicked her. And then think again how good you felt when you decided to do just what she wanted and she was so pleased and happy. God could hold us and not let us do things we choose to do. But He wants us to decide to follow Him because we want to. He wants us to love Him and follow Him because we want to and not because we have to. And He wants us to ask Him to get rid of sin in our lives, too, because He loves us so much. And best of all, we know that when we sin and do bad things and are sorry, He loves us so much that He makes it all good and forgets it so we can start over and try again.

Scripture

God, you know how foolish I have been, my offenses are not hidden from you. —Psalm 69:5

How did you come to fall from the heavens, Daystar, son of Dawn? How did you come to be thrown to the ground, you who enslaved the nations? You who used to think of yourself, "I will climb up to the heavens; and higher than the stars of God I will set my throne. I will sit on the Mount of Assembly in the recesses of the north. I will climb to the top of thunder-

clouds, I will rival the Most High." —Isaiah 14:12-15

Then he took a cup, and when he had returned thanks he gave it to them. "Drink all of you from this," he said, "for this is my blood, the blood of the covenant, which is to be poured out for many for the forgiveness of sins...." —Matthew 26:27, 28

... but however great the number of sins committed, grace was even greater, and so, just as sin reigned wherever there was death, so grace will reign to bring eternal life thanks to the righteousness that comes through Jesus Christ, our Lord. —Romans 5:21

If we say we have no sin in us, we are deceiving ourselves and refusing to admit the truth; but if we acknowledge our sins, then God, who is faithful and just, will forgive our sins and purify us from everything that is wrong. —1 John 1:8-9

Next let me remind you of the angels who had supreme authority but did not keep it and left their appointed sphere.... —Jude 6

Chapter 10

Why Is There a Hell?

Children are fascinated with the idea of sin and guilt and hell and the devil. Fifth graders, in particular, seem bent on keeping any discussion of sin going. I found that it was easy to fall into their trap— the trap of Satan—and discuss sin and evil instead of concentrating on the redemption from sin which came from God through Jesus Christ. And yet the children's longing for safety from evil—for point instead of aimlessness, for beauty instead of ugliness —shines through their discussions like a silver thread. As I pondered the series on evil that the fifth graders' teacher had asked me to do, I suddenly saw a truth that I had never seen before. God uses evil just in the way that an artist uses dark shadows, lines, and forms. His goodness and holiness shine more brightly in contrast to the darkness. Evil was allowed in order to be defeated. If it is in our lives, it is to be defeated there too. "Give these children the tool for defeating evil that God gave: good," the Holy Spirit seemed to be telling me. "Discuss it but be sure that it falls into its proper place in their lives."

So I took up the next week where I had left off discussing the things the children asked for. And I knew in my heart a peace that I had not known before as well as a freedom to discuss the matters of evil without fear. Fear is a tool of the devil, but "perfect love casts out fear." Whose perfect love? Not mine, but God's.

Father, the things we talk about today will be the source of strength for these children for the rest of their lives. Show me what to say. Send your Holy Spirit to instruct them, please.

For the Children

There is a place in Yellowstone Park where hot water bubbles out of a spring. It is so hot that it boils as it comes out, and the mud that it comes through pops like pudding cooking. Imagine that there is a whole lake like that. Imagine that your house is on a hill above that funny lake. You have a nice house and lots of toys and games. You have good things to eat and friends to play with. Your father loves you

very much. Besides, he gives you everything you need and is a fun person to be
with.

Your father likes to have you stay close
to him and do things with him. It seems
like he has so many good ideas that you
never want to be bad. But one day you decide you would like to walk down the path
toward the lake. Your father is in the house
and you walk off without him. Pretty soon
he calls you to come back. Probably you
do. But maybe the next day you walk away
down the path again. Your father calls you
back and you come again. But maybe next
day you get a little farther down the path
and don't hear your father anymore. You
walk on. It is downhill and pretty easy walking. You play along going faster and faster.
Now, you can go back to your father any
time. You can either turn around and go
back or you can call him and he will come
after you. He will even carry you.

As we said, you are free to go back to
your father any time. But suppose you decide not to. You may get nearly down to
the lake and find a new bike on the edge
of the road. If you get on that, you can
go really fast. You might go so fast that
you fall into the lake. Or you might go so
slowly down to the lake that you forget,
almost, that you have a house and father
up on the hill. You might go into the edge

of the water where it isn't so hot and like playing there so much that you never would want to go back to your house and your father. Eventually, you'd be able to swim in the water and finally you would go into it where it was too hot and that would be pretty bad.

When you asked me to come and talk to you about what hell is like, I asked the Holy Spirit to help me tell you what you need to know. Do you think I have forgotten what I came for and have gotten off on a story about a lake? Well, I haven't. I am really telling you a lot about hell. You have heard people say, "I had a little bit of hell that day" and things like that. They are talking about one thing and that thing is getting away from your Father, who is God. As long as we love our Father, God, and stay close to Him, we have all we need and lots and lots of good things besides. But when we get away from Him, we get on a road that slopes down to a very bad end—like the hot lake.

There are some other things, though, that we need to remember about hell. One is that sometimes the way down that sloping path to the lake has things on it that are a lot of fun. When I said that you found a bike and started to ride, I was talking about that. The bike itself wasn't bad. Your father probably gave you a bike up at the house. But the bike down on the road to the hot lake wasn't a nice one that your own father give you. It was one that a bad spirit called the devil gave you to help you go faster on a bad trip away from God. Fun isn't bad. Your Father, God, wants you to have fun and be happy all the time. But He wants you to do it with Him where you are safe.

Hell isn't made up. The Bible tells us several times that it is real as real. Before Jesus came, people talked a lot about hell. After Jesus came, He talked about it, too. But when He died and then rose again, He showed us that that bad place doesn't have any power over Him. He could go right in there and come out again without being hurt at all because He is a part of God himself and nothing is going to hurt Him. So the way to be sure that you will never get lost from your Father by accident or on purpose is to ask Jesus to come into your life and protect you forever from falling into the lake.

Scripture

May the wicked return to Sheol, all the nations forgetful of God. —Psalm 9:17

Sinners in Zion are struck with horror and fear seizes on the godless. Which of us can live with this devouring fire, which of us exist in everlasting flames? —Isaiah 33:14

The Son of Man will send his angels and they will gather out of his kingdom all things that provoke offenses and all who do evil and throw them into the blazing furnace, where there will be weeping and grinding of teeth.—Matthew 13:42

Then Death and Hades were thrown into the burning lake. This burning lake is the second death; and anybody whose name could not be found written in the book of life was thrown into the burning lake.—Revelation 20:14, 15

Chapter 11

Is the Devil Real?

"My dad says the devil isn't real."

I have come to the fifth grade for their final discussion on the forces of evil. They had listened and responded well to the other two, and I had intended to gloss over any more focus on darkness. The devil loves for us to concentrate on him just as much as he loves for us to ignore him and refuse to recognize the havoc he is capable of causing. A position between the two poles is important for fifth graders with their either/or philosophy. But Jesus conquered the devil. By focusing on Him, we can avoid the pitfalls of either ignoring evil or participating in it. So I had prepared a lesson quite different from the one that seemed to be facing me.

One of the hardest lessons teachers have to learn is *when* to throw away the prepared plans. And one of the even harder lessons is *how* to throw them away. One's head is not usually full of creative alternatives on the level of any given grade, and there is nothing so poisonous as an hour of stammering and groping for ideas. Children get out of hand, parents fret, and the teacher loses her self-respect. I am learning, slowly—because the habit of lack-of-trust is much ingrained—to ask the Holy Spirit to speak through me. And I am seeing the need for another lesson: believing in the words I hear coming from me. Most churches have doctrine. Ours doesn't. We are liberal in all interpretations. One pastor may be more fundamental than another, but there is no "standard doctrine" among the teachers of the class, and even less among the children's families. I used to wonder about that. I used to almost envy the person who could say, "I don't know. I'll ask the pastor," when asked a question like the one the fifth grader had presented. But I have learned to say, "I'll ask the Spirit" and be equally satisfied with the answer I receive.

Lord, tell the children about your adversary whom you have defeated.

For the Children

Before we can answer the questions you have asked, we have to see if we can decide something: what is "real"? We know these chairs and tables are real because we can see them and feel them. We can't hear them, though, or smell them, usually. They may have a slight odor, but you can't say, "This is for sure a chair because it smells like one." How do we know the wind is "real"? We can't see it. What we see is what the wind does. It moves things and throws things. But you don't see the wind itself. You don't hear it, either. You hear what it does with tree branches and the shingles on your house or the snow or the sand. And you can't smell it. It may bring a smell from the hamburger place down the street. But you can't say, "Wind smells like hamburger." But you can feel it. It touches your face and your arms and your hair. You say, "The wind is real. I feel it."

Now let's take something else. Do you think love is real? Can you see it? Can you hear it? Can you touch or smell it? Does it touch your cheeks or your hair? Sometimes your mother touches you when she is loving you and you feel that. But that is like the wind. You are seeing what love does instead of seeing it with your eyes or tasting it with your tongue.

There is a place where you feel love, though. It is inside. We won't say where inside, like your stomach or your nose. The

Bible says "your heart," but that only means somewhere inside in the most important place. You feel love so strongly there inside that you do things because of it. You kiss your baby sister or you help your grandfather or you write a poem. You smile and hug someone, or you cry because you wish your puppy hadn't died. You miss your friend who is gone so you don't know what to do with yourself. Those are things—and there are lots more—that you do because you feel love. You can say, "Love is real. I feel it." But you don't know, still, what it looks like.

God is love and Jesus, remember, is God the way your hand is you and is still a hand. So whatever you can say about feeling love, you can also say about feeling or, as the Bible says, "knowing" Jesus. You can see Him in your mind sometimes, but not always. But you can always feel Him inside. And best of all, you can tell that He is there by what He is doing: how He helps you act in loving ways that you could never think of on your own. You can say, "Jesus is real because I know Him."

Now about the devil. You know that sometimes you are bad when you wish you wouldn't be. You think nasty thoughts and say and do ugly things that you didn't like at all. You also see bad things happening all around you. There is sickness and all kinds of hurting things happen to people that you are quite sure a loving God didn't do to them. So you can see, just like you see the trees moving when the wind blows, that there is something bad around. You can't see a little man with horns and a forked tail running around doing bad. But you can see the results of the bad, just the same. That is how you know it is there. We call that badness "the devil" because it is real.

There are a lot of things about the devil that it is a good thing to know. One is that he is a coward. He is afraid of Jesus. He knows that when Jesus died on the cross and then didn't stay dead, Jesus showed him that love is bigger and smarter and better than badness and will finally beat him, no matter what he does. The devil is smart. He was once a very beautiful angel, and while he was with God, he learned a lot of things about everything in the world. So he has lots of sneaky tricks. He likes to make us think that he isn't real, so we won't say "Get out of here in the name of Jesus" to him. He likes to make us worry about him and think about him a lot. That makes him feel powerful. He likes to make us worry about everything. God's love keeps us from worrying, so we can't really think about God's love and worry at the same time.

The devil is real and he is smart and he sometimes bothers us and causes us trouble. But he is a scaredy-cat who can't ruin our lives when we have Jesus inside. All we ever have to do to make the devil go away is tell him to go "in the name of Jesus."

What does "in the name of Jesus" mean? You know that a policeman is just an ordinary man. If he shouted, "Stop in the name of the law," at you when he was standing on the Post Office steps in his blue jeans, nobody would listen to him. Most of the people would laugh at him. But if he had on his policeman's uniform with a gun strapped to his side, everyone around the Post Office would stop if he shouted. What is the difference? He is still the same man. The difference is that, in the name of the law, he has the power to make everyone stop. If they didn't stop by themselves, he could shoot them, if he had to for some very important reason. The state gives him that power. It is like that with us. If we are doing the work of Jesus, then we have His power to make it happen. We never can use His power to make what we decide to do happen. That would be like the policeman in his blue jeans. But part of Jesus' work has always been to stop evil (or the devil), so when we are doing that work we have His uniform on and His power is strapped to our belts. When we shout, "Stop in the name of Jesus," the devil stops.

As we said before, the devil is pretty sneaky. He gets at us in all kinds of ways. But he can never get the best of us for long. He is too afraid of the name of Jesus. That gives us our clue for how to deal with the devil. Whenever we think there is something going on that might not be good, but might be bad instead, we can call on the name of Jesus. Just like that: "Jesus!" Then we can see right away what is happening. Jesus was called "the light of the world" because wherever He is you can see things. The devil likes darkness so he can hide. But Jesus brings light so nothing is hidden. Do you think we are talking about light like sunshine or the light bulb? No, we are talking about the kind of light that is inside you when you know for sure about something. Suppose I asked you, "What is two plus two?" You would know right away. But if I asked you, "What is 237 and 559?", you would have a dark kind of feeling in your mind until you got a pencil and wrote the numbers down—and if you weren't very good in arithmetic, you might still have that dark feeling about the answer you got. That is the kind of light I was talking about. The devil likes that dark feeling and stays in it whenever he can. But Jesus makes it go away. Worry and fear and meanness like to stay in the dark with the devil, but when Jesus comes, those things go away. And Jesus always comes when we call for Him. He told us that in the Bible. It is a promise.

Scripture

He showed me Joshua the high priest, standing before the angel of Yahweh, with Satan standing on his right to accuse him.—Zechariah 3:1

So Yahweh said to Satan, "Where have you been?" "Around the earth," he answered, "roaming about."—Job 1:7

He [Jesus] said to them, "I watched Satan fall like lightning from heaven."—Luke 10:18

"Now sentence is being passed on this world; now the prince of this world is to be overthrown . . . "—John 12:31

Finally, grow strong in the Lord, with the strength of his power. Put God's armour on so as to be able to resist the devil's tactics.—Ephesians 6:10-11

. . . Satan himself goes disguised as an angel of light.—2 Corinthians 11:14

Chapter 12

What Does "Redemption" Mean?

Children like new words. They like the sound and the feel of phrases in their mouths. So when the class started chanting the new word "redemption," I knew they were only enjoying its sound. At least I hoped that is what they were doing. Third and fourth graders can be entirely joyous with tongue-rolling chants and be bored and even offended if someone tries to intellectualize what they are saying. But since I have gotten acquainted with the power and the infinite caring of our Lord, I have noticed that whenever He lets something get started in one of His children, it is for a purpose. Or maybe it is for several purposes. Most of the children I was teaching had been in my class all year. I had substituted and helped in most of the first six grades. The children knew me and we had a happy, unrestrained friendship. If I asked them, they would tell me whether or not they were serious about the hard-for-grown-ups concept of redemption. I opened my mouth to ask them when "something" stopped me. The Holy Spirit is a gentleman. He never presses or manipulates. He leaves me free to hear or to ignore Him. The joy of responding to His tender touch on my shoulder, however, is a full and overwhelming happiness. "Yes, Lord?"

A child in my class had brought a visitor. She might easily have been picked from a garbage can. Her clothes were soiled and ill-fitting and her hair looked as if she had slept several nights on it without combing it. But her eyes had a splendid glow. They asked and longed, and I felt the endless attraction that holiness has for all ages being expressed in her face as she listened. She wasn't playing with a word. She was desperate with a holy desperation for an understanding. Why? What, in her short life, had triggered her need to understand such a grown-up concept? Who knows? Only He himself could answer that. But for her, I led the children from a word game into a learning game. And maybe nobody in the room heard what was said, except my visiting angel.

Lord, your ways are not my ways.

For the Children

It is hard for us to imagine being a slave. Being somebody's slave is like being somebody's horse. You belong to another person, and you can't decide what you are going to do yourself at all. The other person decides—and you have to do it no matter what time it is or how you feel or anything. It used to be, in Bible days and for a long time after that, that when one country lost a war, the other country took most of its people to be slaves. It was just as if you won a fight and for winning, you got to take your opponent's horses to keep for your own. Only instead of horses, we are talking about people. See if you can imagine that you belong to someone. He has a whip and he tells you to get a cloth and wash his feet. Then he tells you to get his clothes and dress him. Maybe when he is dressed he goes outside and watches you while you pile up all the rocks in his backyard. After you are done you have to fix his supper and give it to him and wash the dishes and maybe work some more before you can have your supper. And maybe the only food that is left for you is not very good and there isn't quite enough. But if you don't do your work or if you complain—or maybe if the man who owns you is just mean, he whips you with his whip. Life is pretty hard without much fun in it.

Let's pretend some more. Let's pretend that there are just thousands of rules for everything you do and even think inside your head. There are so many you can't remember them all and you couldn't do them all if you could remember. Your master is standing over you with a whip. Every time you break a rule, he makes you pick up a rock and put it in a big basket you have on your back. You never get to empty the basket and it gets heavier and heavier. Pretty soon you can hardly carry it and you begin to wonder what will happen to you if you get it so heavy you can't move. But no matter what you do, you keep breaking rules and have to keep putting rocks in you basket.

Now let's pretend that a nice man comes along and says to your master, "I will pay you for that slave so you can give him to me. I will pay so much that you will be glad to sell him and I want him." Your master takes the man's money and gives you to him. Now pretend that the first thing the nice man does after you belong to him is to empty your basket and throw it away.

"I have paid for you and I don't want you collecting rocks anymore," he tells you. "I paid a high enough price for you that I can do whatever I want with you. So now you are free. You don't have to collect rocks and you can choose whatever you want to do. But if you want to come with me, I

will love you and take good care of you."
He smiles at you with such a sweet smile
that you love him right away and go with
him happily. But he doesn't make you. He
doesn't carry a whip, and if you decide to
go some other direction, he will not come
after you and beat you.

That is all a made-up story, of course.
It doesn't even sound logical. But if you
looked deep inside yourself, you would be
surprised to find out that you can really
be a slave like that. You can be a slave
to doing a lot of things that you wish you
wouldn't do and to forgetting a lot of the
good, happy things that you know to do.
And every time you do something you are
sorry for or that is bad, you can feel a
little as if you have picked up a rock and
put it in your basket. Probably you your-
selves aren't like that, after all. Because
when Jesus gave His life on the cross, He
paid the high price to get you away from
your old master and make you belong to
Him, and if you know about that, then you
belong to Him and aren't collecting bad
things in a basket.

Do you know what we were doing? We
were explaining that hard old word "redemption." "Redeemed" means that we
have given something and gotten something
back. When you take a quarter to the store
and get a candy bar for it, you have "re-

deemed" the candy bar. When Jesus paid for your life by dying on the cross, He bought or redeemed you. If you had really had a basket of big rocks on your back when He bought you, He would have bought the basket and the rocks, too. That is the way He did it: whatever you have with you, He got when He paid for you. Then if it was something no good, like bad things you had done, He threw it away.

Now Jesus did that buying all at once and ever since it is done for everyone. That is a mystery we don't understand. But the Bible says it is true and sure enough, if we ask Jesus to be our Master, He will take all our bad things and throw them away. We still may make mistakes and do wrong things, of course, because He didn't make puppets out of us. But He is such a good Master that instead of collecting all our mistakes in baskets, we can give each one to Him and He will forgive us and either throw the mistake away or make something good out of it.

Scripture

Let Israel rely on Yahewh as much as the watchman on the dawn! For it is with Yahweh that mercy is to be found, and a generous redemption; it is he who redeems Israel from all their sins.—Psalm 130:7, 8

No; anyone who wants to be great among

you must be your servant, and anyone who wants to be first among you must be your slave, just as the Son of Man came not to be served but to serve, and to give his life as a ransom for many.—Matthew 20:26-28

You are not your own property; you have been bought and paid for.—1 Corinthians 6:20

He sacrificed himself for us in order to set us free from all wickedness and to purify a people so that it could be his very own and we would have no ambition except to do good.—Titus 2:14

Chapter 13

How Did the World Begin?

The third graders were playing with clay. Billy was pretending to be God.

"Wham!" he said, clapping the clay in his hands. "I've just made the world." Becky laughed.

"It took God six days to make the world."

"God didn't really make the world in six days. The Bible just says that because the Bible's just a story."

"He made it in steps, and I know what they are." Dorothy had won a Bible in a memorization contest.

"What about dinosauers? I'll bet there wasn't room on the ark for many of them."

The questions went on. Did they really want to know? Were they just playing? I had no prepared lesson on creation. I had no set ideas on creation. I believed the Bible, and I hadn't really ever tried to square it with the science of anthropology. Yet I recognized the children's need—the need we all have to feel the security of knowing God's hand on our lives. The ancient people who finally got the even more ancient stories down on paper had succeeded in conveying their clear concept of both God's power and His compassion. Did they have anything to say to my modern friends, the third graders?

Those children had been indoctrinated with the religion of science. To them and their parents before them, there could be no other gods before science. One does not lightly do anything to dethrone a god. And yet I myself did not believe that scientists had come up with answers that adequately relegated the Bible story of creation to the trash. This was a moment I could gloss over quickly or make use of. The teacher's everpresent dilemma in Sunday school is to decide which moment to use and which to let slip by. But the Holy Spirit seemed to be pressing me forward to speak.

For the Children

There is one thing that nobody knows much about. Not even the best scientists have ever completely figured it out. That is how the world began. The only place we have any records about what happened is in the Bible. The people who wrote the Bible lived a long, long time ago. And everything they wrote had been told by the fathers to their children a long time before that, besides. This doesn't mean that those stories were made up, though. It just means that what they said doesn't sound like science-lab in your room at school. So let's get our Bibles out and see what we can find out about the beginning of the world.

You all know that there are lots of stars and planets and meteorites in space—and that there is a great deal of space. Nobody can really understand all that space, and nobody ever could. The people who wrote the Bible called it "the heavens." I guess that's good enough for us. The thing that is important is that God has always been in charge of "the heavens." It's a good thing, too. Only God could keep everything in order when it is all so complicated. He knows and has always known exactly what He was doing. Scientists talk about all of their different ideas to try to explain how our world and the other worlds came into being. They can't decide. That is all right. We know that God made our world because He wanted to—and that was a good enough reason.

When we look in the Bible, we find out that God didn't just snap His fingers and make the world all at once. He did it a step at a time. And if we look at the Bible, we see that they were very sensible steps. He didn't make anybody to start living here until He had a good, comfortable place for them to live and plenty of food and water. God made all the rules himself, so of course He followed them. His rules are always logical. That is why we know what to expect— like one day and then one night instead of two nights in a row; or a carrot coming up when we plant a carrot seed and not, for instance, a crocodile.

At first the earth didn't have any shape and it was dark and wet. So the first thing God did was to make it light. We can imagine Him taking a handful of this dark wetness and setting it over in the light. It must have looked pretty, because the Bible says, "God saw that it was good." (Have you ever been looking at a perfectly clear piece of blue sky when suddenly a little fluffy cloud appeared? It was a happy surprise, wasn't it?) That was the first thing God did, and the Bible says it was the first day. People often get into quarrels over that section because scientists know that each part of creation took a long, long time. They sometimes forget, I guess, that nobody ever said how long a day used to be in those days. There are two places in the Bible which tell us that with God a day is like a thousand years. So we don't have to get into that quarrel.

The next thing God did was to make what we call "the atmosphere." That's the air we breathe which goes all around the earth. He divided that off from the big mass that was just a blob of wetness before that. Each time God did something new, the Bible says, "God saw that it was good." How do you suppose the people who wrote the Bible knew how God felt? I have a guess. Have you ever been so pleased with something you were making that you just fairly jumped with joy? I think most of us have. That's how we can guess how God felt while He was making the world.

Next, God put the water together for oceans. That let the land come out and be dry. So He put all kinds of plants everywhere. That was what the Bible says happened on the third day. Scientists can find crooked rocks and all kinds of signs that there was a terrific upheaval when God pushed the mountains up out of the water. That was a big day in the life of our world. Don't you imagine it shook and trembled for a long time after that? When the earth shakes just the tiniest bit, we notice it. We call it an earthquake. I'll guess those first earthquakes were really big ones.

On the fourth day, God cleared things up so the moon and stars showed and started the earth going around so the sun would show in the daytime and the stars and moon at night. That fixed it so all the plants would get some sunshine. There is where the Bible says days and nights got started. You can see why it was so hard to count time in those days, can't you? We don't know how long it took for a day when days first began.

The fifth day must have been an exciting day. God made birds and creatures of all kinds. He put them everywhere—in the ocean and on the land. Some were large and some were small. He didn't put on some of the animals we know now, though. If we look carefully at the Bible, we'll see that those first ones were called "birds, living creatures, and serpents." I guess some of those bones that we look at in museums, that we call "prehistoric monsters," were made on that day. And we still don't know how long each day lasted, compared to days now. We do know, though, that the next thing God did was to make cattle and horses—the kinds of animals we know—and also on that sixth day He made man.

If we look at the Bible some more, we'll find some interesting things about man. God took up a little bit of dust and then breathed His Spirit into him to make him alive. The name "Adam" means "of the soil," in the language the Bible was written in. So Adam came from the dirt; but by breathing His own Spirit into him, God made him different from all the other animals. Man can know God and love Him and want to be friends with Him. Although God loves all the animals in His world, they don't know how to be His special friends the way we do.

The Bible says that God made man in His own image. That means that He gave us all the kind of love and bravery and humor and loyalty that He has. We don't have as much of those good things as He has; but we have enough to make us know how good and great and happy we *could* be. We also have enough to make us want to know God better.

God put Adam in a very beautiful place called "The Garden of Eden." There was everything in that garden that he could think of to eat and drink and do. There was one thing missing, though. You could think of it if you tried. Adam was lonesome. He needed someone to do things with and to talk to. You know how hard it would be to play alone all the time, no matter how nice a garden you had. So God put Adam to sleep and made Eve out of his rib. Eve was the first woman just like Adam was the first man. God told them they could tame all the animals and give them names. He told them to live in the garden and have a family and be happy. The Bible says, "God saw all he had made, and indeed it was very good." You can imagine how much He loved Adam and Eve and all the plants and animals if you think how pleased you were about the very best thing you ever made, can't you? We can only make things out of what God has given us. God made the world and everything in it out of nothing—except Adam. He was made of dust, remember.

There was one more day. It was the seventh day. That was the day God rested after all the work He had done. He not only rested himself, but the Bible says "God blessed the seventh day and made it holy ...." What do you suppose that means?

God made a lot of good rules. We talked a while ago about planting a carrot seed and getting a carrot for sure and not something else, like maybe a crocodile. When something is tossed up, it falls down. That is gravity, and it is a very good idea, too. When our astronauts got out into space, they found out how hard it is not to have the kind of gravity they were used to on the ground. So God made another good rule —that it is good to rest after a week's work. The best way to rest is to turn to God. So He said that once a week it would be important to turn to Him and get rested. When we call something "holy" we mean turned-to-God. It's not something we have to do because God said we should, as much as something He made us want to do because we love Him.

There is a lot we will probably never know about the beginning of our world. We don't need to worry about how He made the world. We can just enjoy living here and help take care of it.

Scripture

Genesis 1:1 to 2:9 was used as the background for the entire lesson. In addition:

To you, a thousand years are a single day, a yesterday now over, an hour of the night. —Psalm 90:4

Let the whole world fear Yahweh, let all who live on earth revere him! He spoke, and it was created; he commanded and there it stood. — Psalm 33:8, 9

But there is one thing, my friends, that you must never forget: that with the Lord, "a day" can mean a thousand years, and a thousand years is like a day. —2 Peter 3:8

Chapter 14

Where Is Heaven?

Small children never seem to wonder about heaven. I guess they are so enthralled and mystified with the discovery of this world that another dimension doesn't seem possible to them. Or perhaps they have so recently come from there that they don't need to wonder. In any case, although I tried periodically, I never succeeded in getting my kindergartners interested. And perhaps it was just as well. I was caught in a trap I think many people are. We think of heaven as being something totally different from what we experience here. We think of the descriptions, the prophecies, the hints that we receive from the Bible as indicating an experience entirely foreign to the one we're in now. And, whether we mean to or not, when we think "different" we think "unreal."

I wasn't really prepared one day for the requirement of explaining heaven to a group of 5th, 6th, and 7th graders who had gathered for a handcraft session in Bible school.

"I wouldn't like heaven," one youngster stated emphatically. We all looked at her in surprise. Her reasons, stated clearly and with feeling, expressed many remarks I'd heard from adults.

"I wouldn't want to sit around and sing praises to God all day."

"Jewels are pretty but they don't mean anything. Streets of gold would be boring."

"What would there be to do? I'd be bored spending forever there."

I could see her points. Our modern world is full of excitement. There's lots to do. The child wasn't hungry or cold, ill, or neglected. How could heaven compete with cars and television and pretty clothes, boy friends, Coca-Cola and ham sandwiches? Holy Spirit, help me. Again, help me, please.

For the Children

Let's begin by throwing out all our old ideas about heaven and beginning over. Let's see what singing praises to God and jewels and golden streets would mean if we changed them into things we really do care for.

Let's think, really think, about the happiest times we've ever had. What made them happy? Often we were making something that was really fun to make—that was turning out right and promising to be a real success. We felt good and useful, smart and successful. Chalk up one for how it'll be in heaven. We are sons of God, through His son, Jesus. We then are His heirs. That means we have what He has. We have the materials to make things, and since there is absolutely no evil in heaven to mess up what we are doing, the things we make will always be successful.

Happy times usually involve someone else. Even when we are all alone, we need to know that we have someone who cares, waiting to share with us. Sharing and doing things together make us happy. It is lots more fun to find the biggest toadstool or the smoothest rock if we can share it with someone who is interested. Or, supposing we know a very funny joke. Isn't it terrible not to know *anyone* to tell it to? Chalk up another point for heaven. We are brothers and sisters in Christ and in heaven we will have the companionship of people we love to share with and enjoy. Without evil, we will never quarrel and will be always understanding and kind to each other.

Have you ever had a dog or a cat that you loved get killed or become sick and die? Have you ever had a grandmother or a brother or a friend whom you loved die? Did you ever know a really nice person whom you cared for who was sick? In heaven there will be no dying, sickness or sorrow. You will not have to watch your dear old grandfather get weak and sick and finally die, because in heaven death will be gone. You will not cry because you will never be sad. And the animals will not kill each other, either. Most of us have at some time rescued a little bird or a baby squirrel and then seen the cat catch it. Most of us have been sad to watch one animal sneak up on another one and catch it, kill it, and eat it. That kind of sadness won't happen in heaven. The Bible says, "The lion shall lie down with the lamb." Lambs are food for lions in this world. But in heaven nothing has to kill anything.

Another thing: have you ever been having a wonderful time doing something just perfect and suddenly looked at the clock only to discover that it was time to go? Oh how you hated to leave! But in heaven, there is no time. Can you imagine that, instead of going on hour after hour, day after day, time just didn't exist anymore? It's hard to imagine that; but when men flew out into space they showed us how it was possible to fly with the sun so they never had morning or evening. In the Bible it says, "With God a thousand years is like a day. . . ." That means we won't have to worry about time in heaven. If we're busy building something very beautiful, we can just keep building as long as we want to.

Music and color, the nice feel of things, tastes, shapes, textures all are of this world but promise to be in the next. Paul said that all creation is waiting to be born again all perfect. All of the people who love Jesus will have perfect bodies and so will the world. So all of the already lovely things, which are now not perfect, will not go away but will instead become even more perfect. Even those of us who have squeaky voices here will probably be able to sing in heaven.

Have you ever wished you looked better? Most of us have. But you wouldn't like to be *entirely* different so nobody would know you. Paul said when we get to heaven we'll put off our bodies that are imperfect and put on ones that are perfect. But they'll be enough like the ones we have so we'll know each other. Won't that be nice? perfect bodies?

The best part of heaven will be being with Jesus all the time. The people who knew Him when He was here, loved to be with Jesus whenever they could. Can you think of anyone you really like to be with? Imagine the very happiest time you ever had with the person you loved most in the world and then imagine how happy you'd be if you could go do that same thing with that same person again—only have it be a hundred times nicer. We get little glimpses of how good it'll be to be in the presence of Jesus, whenever we feel completely happy with someone whom we love a great deal. But then something comes along to spoil it. In heaven, nothing will ever spoil it.

Now what about the jewels and the golden streets and the singing praises? Well, as you know, a jewel is something both beautiful and valuable. If you had one you would take very good care of it. If you loved someone *very* much, you might give it to him. The word "jewel" is often used to express goodness. Have you ever heard your mother say, "My she was a good girl. She was just a jewel." Now obviously, the good girl did not suddenly turn into a colored rock. Mother was just saying that to put across the idea that her girl was both beautiful and precious. When the writers of the Bible wanted to say, quickly, how beautiful heaven will be, they said, "It is full of jewels." If we think of each of the good things we mentioned a while ago as being something very precious, we might easily say, "Heaven is full of jewels. And it's so special even the streets are gold"—just because gold is something valuable and beautiful, too.

Now we come to singing praises. That really does sound dull. But lets change it around a bit. Suppose your dad did something just super nice and special. You'd probably say, "Gee, Dad, that was great. You sure are smart. Thanks." You were singing praises. You were praising your dad and thanking him. Now suppose he kept on doing neat things all evening, one after the other, until bedtime. You said "thank you" several times! But when bedtime came and Daddy tucked you in, you felt as if you just had to tell him, somehow, that you thought he had been a super good dad and you loved him. It wasn't boring. It was acting out the good, happy way you felt. "Singing praises to God" is just the way the people who wrote the Bible expressed telling a great Guy that He had sure been nice to them. You won't *have* to do it. You'll want to.

When you fall in love you'll understand that part better. When people fall in love, they spend lots of time looking into each others' eyes and saying, "You're wonderful. I love you." To the rest of us, saying that over and over seems pretty tiresome. But they feel that way, so they aren't bored. In heaven, God will be so wonderful that we'll feel like saying so. He won't make us. We'll enjoy it.

Scripture

The spirit himself and our spirit bear united witness that we are children of God. And if we are children we are heirs as well: heirs of God and coheirs with Christ, sharing his sufferings so as to share His Glory.—Romans 8:17

... and the dead will be raised, imperishable, and we shall be changed as well, because our present perishable nature must put on imperishability and this mortal nature must put on immortality.—1 Corinthians 15:53

From the beginning till now the entire creation, as we know, has been groaning in one great act of giving birth; and not only creation, but all of us who possess the firstfruits of the Spirit, we too groan inwardly as we wait for our bodies to be set free.—Romans 8:22, 23

... those who have died in Christ will be the first to rise, and then those of us who are still alive will be taken up in the clouds, together with them, to meet the Lord in the air. So we shall stay with the Lord for ever.—1 Thessalonians 4:17

But there is one thing, my friends, that you must never forget: that with the Lord, "a day" can mean a thousand years, and a thousand years is like a day. —2 Peter 3:8

Be glad and rejoice for ever and ever for what I am creating, because I now create Jerusalem "joy" and her people "gladness."... No more will the sound of weeping or the sound of cries be heard.... Long before they call I shall answer; before they stop speaking I shall have heard. The wolf and the young lamb will feed together, the lion eat straw like the ox, ...

*They will do no hurt, no harm on all my holy
mountain, says Yahweh.*—Isaiah 65:17-25

*You see this city? Here God lives among
men. He will make his home among them; they
shall be his people, and he will be their God;
his name is God-with-them. He will wipe away
all tears from their eyes; there will be no more
death, and no more mourning or sadness....
Then the One sitting on the throne spoke: "Now
I am making the whole of creation new," he
said.* —Revelation 21:3-6

*The foundations of the city wall were faced
with all kinds of precious stone:... and the
main street of the city was pure gold.*—Revelation 21:19-22

*They all had harps from God, and they were
singing the hymn of Moses, the servant of God,
and of the Lamb:*

*"How great and wonderful are all your works,
Lord God Almighty; just and true are all
your ways, King of nations. Who would not
revere and praise your name, O Lord? You
alone are holy, and all the pagans will come
and adore you for the many acts of justice
you have shown."*—Revelation 15:3-4

Chapter 15

Why Is Tommy So Mean?

Mike was a great little boy. He was sweet and creative, always took part in our activities and discussions, and, in general, was a kindergarten teacher's dream-come-true. But one day he was naughty. The contrast with his usual behavior nearly undid the whole class. He was smarty, noisy, destructive—wouldn't listen or cooperate. After he had at least a third of his classmates in tears, I finally did what I should have done sooner: I prayed.

"Lord, tell me what to do. How can I solve the riddle that Mike has become and restore my class to productivity?" Peace filled me. My tension left. I looked at Mike again and saw the worry lines across his forehead, the tears bright behind his blue eyes. I walked over to him.

"Sit down, everyone," I said firmly,

taking Mike onto my lap. "Mike has trouble. Let's see how we can help him." The children responded, as usual, with grace and compassion. They sat down quietly, serious in the face of an emergency.

"Now tell us, Mike, why you are unhappy today?" The children leaned forward. Mike buried his face in my blouse.

"Mommy doesn't like me." A sob shook him. "Mommy doesn't like *any* five-year-old. She says it's a bad age." His grief turned to a wail and Beth patted him tenderly. We sat in silence while he grew quiet, and then I began to talk to Mike, and to the other children, and to myself, and to all of us who are troubled by the destructive naughtiness that fills our society. I could tell by their warmth and the enthusiasm of their responses that I had been given a tool to help children of all ages to cope, not only with the meanness of their peers, but also with difficult teachers and parents.

We started a project that morning that lasted until the end of my teaching days. We started what we called our "Good Doctor" project. The children would bring tales of meanness by their peers and I would say, "And what did the Good Doctor do?" Gradually they learned to respond, first in Sunday school, and I believe later, with encouragement, in their home and school situations. They learned to think of loving the person even while hating his acts. They learned to at least try to find the unhappiness that perpetrated the meanness. Of course no one is always at his best. They quarreled and fought and hit back. But even so, I often heard them say,

"I wonder how I can help Tommy be happier so he won't be so mean."

Thank you, Holy Spirit, for your never-failing wisdom.

For the Children

Some days the sun shines outside and we feel all happy and warm inside. Breakfast tastes just right. Mommy looks pretty and little brother is fun to play with. Those are good days. Hardly anybody can be naughty on a good day.

Then there are bad days. Lots of things make bad days. Sometimes we know what they are—like a cough or a tummy ache—and sometimes we don't know. On the "don't know" days, things just go wrong. Suppose you heard your mother and father talking about you growing so fast you needed new shoes. Then they said there wasn't enough money. All of a sudden you were mad at yourself for growing so fast. And besides that, you were worried about the shoes and the money. That might turn into a very bad day. Because when we're worried, we're cross, and when we're cross we usually do naughty things. It always helps to ask Jesus to come and help us feel better. But sometimes we forget; and some people don't know that Jesus loves us and will help us quickly when we ask Him.

Now let's pretend. Let's pretend that Mommy is having a bad day. Mommy is worried and cross and she grumps at the whole family. Little sister doesn't like to hear Mommy grump, so she throws her cereal on Mike. That makes Mike have to change his clothes and that makes him late for Sunday school. How do you suppose he will act in Sunday school? You guessed it! He will be naughty. He will poke Mary and Sue and take George's blocks away from him. He will remember that Mommy said five is a bad age and he is five so he will feel very sad and cross and bad. Mike needs a good doctor. Lord Jesus, come and be our good doctor.

The first thing a good doctor does is make an examination. He looks at your tongue and your ears and listens to you breathe. Now the Good Doctor is looking at Mike. He sees that Mike is not sick. He is fine. He can write his name and tie his shoes and read the hours on the clock. He makes his bed, feeds his cat, and is careful with his baby sister. Mike is very healthy.

Then, Lord Jesus, why is Mike being so naughty?

Mike is being naughty today because he has a worry. He thinks his Mommy doesn't like him. So what we need to do is see if this bad day is caused by poor Mommy having a trouble. Mommies love their children. They know that sometimes children have bad days. But they like them at every age. Mike's Mommy said that because she had a bad day herself. How can Mike cure his troubles? He can be very kind and sympathetic with his Mommy and help her feel better, because she is the one who is having trouble.

Now we can pretend again. There is a boy at school who hits and pokes and steals caps. Nobody will play with him because he is so bad. There are several things we can do. We can hit and poke him and steal his cap. We can run away from him and never play with him. Or we can call the Good Doctor and get Him to help. What do you think the Good Doctor will do? He will look that boy all over and find out what is making him unhappy. He will see if he is worried or sick or afraid. Then He will help the rest of the children in his class to be kind and understanding and loving to him because he has a trouble.

There's another kind of bad-day maker. It's a funny one, but it causes a lot of trouble. It takes a Good Doctor to figure it out. Let's pretend one more time. Let's pretend that when Mike was a little tiny boy still wearing diapers, his daddy spanked him very hard for touching something he wasn't supposed to touch. Let's say it was little glass animals. Now he's five years old and he gets very naughty every time he sees little glass animals. It makes him act like a little tiny boy. Sometimes when someone hurts you it is because something you did makes him feel like a little tiny boy. If you act like a little tiny boy, too, then it can easily become a bad day. That's when we need to, quick, call the Lord Jesus and ask Him to help everybody grow back up.

Whenever someone is mean and hurts someone else, it is because he is having trouble. If we ask the Lord Jesus to be there, we can usually help him to make a good day out of a bad day.

Scripture

It is not the healthy who need the doctor, but the sick.—Matthew. 9:12

You must want love more than anything else, . . .—1 Corinthians 14:1

Let kindliness and loyalty never leave you. —Proverbs 3:3

Do not refuse a kindness to anyone who begs it, if it is in your power to perform it. Do not say to your neighbour, "Go away! Come another time! I will give it to you tomorrow," if you can do it now.—Proverbs 3:27, 28

Resentment and anger, these are foul things, too, . . . —Sirac 27:30

Do not abandon yourself to sorrow, do not torment yourself with brooding. Gladness of heart is life to a man, joy is what gives him length of days.—Sirac 30:21-23

. . . love covers over all offences.—Proverbs 10:12

Chapter 16

How Can I Thank God for Something Bad?

I tripped on the top step of a long steep flight of wooden stairs and rolled clear to the bottom where I lay moaning amid all my books and papers. As my head cleared, I did what the Holy Spirit had been urging me to do, no matter what. I said, with my eyes still closed, "Thank you, Lord."

The stairway ended in front of the 4th grade room. When I opened my eyes, I was looking up at about a dozen worried 9-year-olds attracted by the crashing. They helped me up and comforted me as only one's beloved friends are able. I went on to my own kindergarten group, aware that I had material for a lesson if I could just get myself together.

The loving concern of my own group undid my already upset self-control and I found myself in tears as I answered their question: "Where did you hurt?" After a bit we got the Bible and had a wonderful extemporaneous lesson on self-acceptance out of Ecclesiastes 3:4. "There is a time to cry and a time to laugh." I thought the matter was over and thanked the Lord that He had been with me, both in the mishap and in the lesson. However, I had not heard the last of it. At the end of the hour the shy little redhead who taught the 4th grade came to talk.

The children, it seemed, had spent most of their time in a heated discussion about thanking God when things go wrong. Some of my ex-kindergartners were defending my doing it, out of loyalty, but most of them were as perplexed by the idea as the adults with whom one had that sort of discussion. Would I exchange a section of my week's hour with her and talk to her class? she asked. I agreed. But how could I explain this concept which is mostly a matter of faith? How could I tell them what I hardly knew myself? It would have to be in the hands of the Holy Spirit—again.

For the Children

Let's pretend that there is a group of 35 Cub Scouts taking a hike. There is a path which goes through a canyon, over rocks, up a hill, down a hill, through a grassy meadow, across a river, and finally ends at a nice big house. The Assistant Scoutmaster leads the way and the Scoutmaster follows along behind.

Up overhead is a cloud and you are sitting on it watching the Scouts hike. You can see where they are going and where they started. You can see who takes a little side trip to climb a tree. You can see who falls down and who eats his sandwich before lunch time. You can see that the Scoutmaster is just walking along, making sure everyone gets there, but he isn't yelling at anybody to stay in line. You can tell about what time they'll get to the ranch house because you can see all the things they're doing.

Wasn't that a funny pretend? Now pretend one more time. Pretend it is God on the cloud watching and each Cub Scout is a little piece of your life. God can see your whole life at once—the beginning and the end. He can see that you are falling over your untied shoelaces, but He doesn't tie them for you. Instead He lets you keep tripping over them until you learn to tie them. That way you don't just stay a baby but grow up. He sees you running off to climb a tree. He knows you will have to hurry to catch up, but He also knows you can do it. He lets you eat your sandwich before lunch and get awfully hungry before supper to help you learn how to work with the rules. And He will call to you and warn you not to fall in the river; but He won't usually snatch you out of the river if you just will not listen to Him. Even though He can see your whole life at once, God is not far off but is very near and loves you very much. He wants to tell you how to have a happy hike. However, you have to know He is there and to listen to Him.

Now we did all that pretending so I could talk to you about thanking God. We know that God can tell what is happening to you every day just the way you, on the cloud, could see all the Cub Scouts at the same time. So He knows that sometimes something that looks bad to you might be very good for you if you could just see your whole life at once. Let's think of an example. Suppose that you got lost in the woods and didn't get back to your house to watch a television program at 4 o'clock. You asked God to show you the way out. But He didn't. He kept telling you not to worry, but you didn't listen. You did worry and were afraid and were even getting pretty mad at God for not answering your prayer. Finally though, at five o'clock, you found your way out of the woods and got home. And you discovered when you got there that your stove had exploded and if you had been there you would have been burned. See how easy it would have been to say "thank you" to God for not bringing you out of the woods when you asked Him to? He knew the reason He didn't rescue you even if you didn't.

Let's make up another story. Suppose you had a white cat that you loved. He got lost. You asked God to bring your kitty back and He did. You said "thank you" and enjoyed your kitty for several days before he got lost again. But you weren't worried. You asked God to bring him back again. Only this time He didn't. It would be hard to say "thank you," wouldn't it? It would be easier if you later found out that there was a little crippled girl who adopted your kitty because she was lonesome and needed a friend. Then you could say "thank you" because God had done the best thing, even though losing your kitty made you sad. We know that God loves us so much He never, never lets us be hurt unless there is some really good reason that He can see and we can't.

Suppose, though, that something happens that really hurts and there doesn't seem to be any reason for it at all. Pretend that you trip on the stairs and fall all the way down to the bottom. Or pretend that you find your kitty dead when you asked God to bring him back. Then it's really hard to say "thank you" to God. He seems like an old meanie, and what happened seems like the worst badness that ever was. That's the time to remember your seat up on the cloud. God can see clear to the end of your life, and He knows what good things are going to happen to you even when you can't see them. He has promised that whatever happens will turn out for good because He loves you so very much. So you can say "thank you" no matter what happens.

Let's pretend one more time. Pretend you have a stomachache. Your mother takes you to the doctor and next thing you know, you wake up with a headache and a sore tummy and even feel like throwing up. You can be very angry and shout at the doctor, "I came to get you to make me well and you made me worse. I'm mad at you!" But if you stop shouting, maybe you'll find out that the doctor saved your life by taking out your appendix. Then you'll say "thank you" even though you still feel very sick. If you ever find out that God always knows what is happening and will always make the bad things that happen turn out for the best, then you can quit worrying, even when you are having a hard time. Then you can say "thank you, God" for everything—even a broken leg.

Scripture

Finally, brothers, rejoice in the Lord. —Philippians 3:1

Be happy at all times; pray constantly; and for all things give thanks to God, because this is what God expects you to do in Christ Jesus. —1 Thessalonians 5:16-19

Your love is better than life itself; my lips will recite your praise; all my life I will bless you, in your name lift up my hands; on my lips a song of joy and, in my mouth, praise. —Psalm 63:3-6

Praise is rightfully yours, God, in Zion. Vows to you must be fulfilled, for you answer prayer. —Psalm 65:1

Sing a new hymn to Yahweh! Let his praise resound from the ends of the earth; let the sea and all that it holds sing his praises, the islands and those who inhabit them. . . .

"But I will make the blind walk along the road and lead them along paths. I will turn darkness into light before them and rocky places into level tracks."—Isaiah 42:10, 16

. . . let us offer God an unending sacrifice of praise, a verbal sacrifice that is offered every time we acknowledge his name.—Hebrews 13:15

Index of Scripture

Chapter 10: Hell

Psalm 9:17
Isaiah 33:14
Matthew 13:42
Revelation 20:15

Chapter 11: The Devil

Zechariah 3:1
Job 1:7
Luke 10:18
John 12:31
Ephesians 6:10-11
2 Corinthians 11:14

Chapter 12: Redemption

Psalm 130:7
Matthew 20:28
1 Corinthians 6:20
Titus 2:14

Chapter 13: Creation

Genesis 1 to 2:9 was used
for the background
Psalm 90:4
Psalm 33:8-9
2 Peter 3:8

Chapter 14: Meanness

1 Corinthians 14:1
Proverbs 3:1
Sirac 27:30
Proverbs 10:12

Chapter 15: Praises to God

Philippians 3:1
1 Thessalonians 5:16-19
Psalm 63:3-6
Psalm 65:1
Isaiah 42:10 and 16
Hebrews 13:15

Chapter 16: Heaven

Romans 8:17
1 Corinthians 15:53
Romans 8:23
1 Thessalonians 4:17
2 Peter 3:8
Isaiah 65:17-26
Revelation 21:3-6
Revelation 21:19-22
Revelation 15:3-5